THE LAW OF

THE NEW THOUGHT

A Study of Fundamental Principles
and Their Application

By WILLIAM WALKER ATKINSON

ASSOCIATE EDITOR OF "NEW THOUGHT," CHICAGO; AUTHOR OF
"THOUGHT FORCE IN BUSINESS AND
EVERYDAY LIFE," ETC.

"O, let not the flame die out! Cherished age after age in its dark caverns, in its holy
temples cherished. Fed by pure ministers of love—let not the flame die out."
                                        —*EDWARD CARPENTER.*

PUBLISHED BY
THE PSYCHIC RESEARCH COMPANY
3835 Vincennes Ave., Chicago, Ill.
1902

CONTENTS.

CHAPTER VIII. THE SUB-CONSCIOUS PLANE......... 45

The greater part of our thinking performed along sub-conscious lines—
Illustrations of this fact—The sub-conscious, the habit plane—Means
by which the sub-conscious mentality is reached—A store-house of
thoughts—A mixture of wisdom and foolishness—How the super-
conscious faculties manifest first along sub-conscious lines—A reservoir receiving conscious thoughts—The desirability of a clear supplying stream—Auto-suggestions and affirmations—Did thought originate on the conscious, or sub-conscious plane?—My views on the
subject—Filling the store-house with proper material—Creating on
the thought plane—Our own thoughts, not others—Disease producing
on the sub-conscious plane—Thoughts take form in action—As a
man thinketh in his heart, so is he.

CHAPTER IX. THE SUPER-CONSCIOUS FACULTIES....... 51

Faculties outside the realm of consciousness—Latent but unfolding—Super-
conscious faculties not a part of a sub-conscious mind, although
often manifested along sub-conscious lines—The distinction between
sub-conscious thoughts and those of the super-conscious faculties—
Above consciousness, not below it—Developing super-conscious faculties—The sub-conscious contains only what has been placed there—
The super-consciousness contains knowledge heretofore unrevealed
to Man—Drawing on the super-consciousness—What the super-
consciousness reveals to Man—What it has revealed—The most important truths come in this way—The higher psychic powers latent
within the super-consciousness—Productions which have "soul" in
them come from the super-conscious faculties—The dwelling place
of the Spirit—The Spirit and its domain—Recognition of the Spirit.

CHAPTER X. THE SOUL'S QUESTION.................. 57

Whence come I? Whither go I? What am I? What is the object of my
existence?—Questions asked in all ages, in this and other worlds—
The question absolutely unanswered for most men—Struggles for
freedom—Climbing the mountain of Knowledge—The task begun,
not ended—The spiritual hunger—Bread, not stones—The want is
the prophecy of the means of satisfying it—The intellect will not
answer the Riddle of the Universe—The answer must come from
within—The Something Within—The development of Spiritual Consciousness—The intelligent Faith which knows, not merely understands—Unexplored regions of the Soul—Not contrary to intellect,
but beyond it—A new world of knowledge opened out before the
mental gaze—Joy insuperable.

CHAPTER XI. THE ABSOLUTE 60

God has begotten the Universe—The Universe has no boundaries or
limits—God manifested in every atom—The Causeless Cause—The
Intellect and its troubles—Man may spiritually know the reality of
God—Man's different concepts of God—God's attributes, Omnipotence, Omniscience and Omnipresence, and their explanation—The
Father-Mother—The apparently conflicting ideas regarding God,
reconciled—God's manifestations: Substance, Energy, and Spirit—

All men really worshiping the one God, although apparently wor-
shiping many—A Personal God without the limitations of personality
—God manifesting in Infinite Spirit—In Infinite Energy—In Infinite
Substance—Man growing in God-consciousness—Nearer, my God, to
Thee—All are children of God, with a share of his attributes.

There is but One—God's manifestations apparently innumerable, but in
reality but One—Universal Oneness—Centre and circumference—
The rays from the Centre reach all parts of the circle—High and
low; beautiful and hideous; exalted or depraved; all a part of the
One—Separateness but an illusion—God the only standard of perfection—Individuality does not decrease but grows—Beginning to understand—Truth everywhere—Sin the result of a belief in separateness
—Invariable laws in operation—The fundamental consciousness of
religion—The Universal Presence—The Oneness of All explains
psychic mysteries, and relationships between persons and things—
Human sympathy growing—The point towards which the race is
traveling.

Man IS, and will be—Life continues—The "I" is the Soul—Higher and
lower forms of life—Life on different planes—Metempsychosis or
Reincarnation—A higher view of the subject—The Soul has existed
for ages—Progressing from lower to higher forms, and still progressing—Theories not fundamental when the consciousness of immortality is reached—Living in the Now—Universal Law—Man's concepts changing as he grows—We are babes in understanding, compared with those who have reached higher planes—Angels and
archangels—The Universe filled with forms of life, in different
stages of development—Man but a manifestation of the Soul in one
particular stage of development—Paul, the mystic, and his view.

Man's development along the lines of unfoldment—The power within—A
mighty force—Developing and unfolding like a plant—Life is growth
Within and Without—The Divine Paradox—Action and reaction—
The internal urge and the external obstacles, both factors in development—Relative and Absolute—The final, or ultimate, effect or
product, is the underlying cause of the unfoldment—Man the effect, is
Man the Cause—In Man of to-day nestles the Higher Man of the
future—The first last, and the last first—Growth always accompanied with pain—Co-operation with the law makes growth less
painful—Folly of opposing growth—The Something Within is pressing for unfoldment.

Consciousness in the lower animals—Mere sensation at first; almost automatic—Growth—Lower form of Consciousness—The development
of Self-consciousness—Definition of Simple Consciousness and Self-
consciousness—The first conception of the "I"—"I" on the physical

CHAPTER I.

"WHAT IS THE 'NEW THOUGHT'?"

The question—Difficult to answer—The New Thought is the oldest thought —Known to the few in all ages—Found at the heart of all religions and philosophies—In the songs of the poets and the writings of the mystics—The flame kept alive through the long ages—Hard sayings and dark corners made clear—The first glimmer of recognition—A great wave of psychic thought now passing over the world—What the New Thought stands for—No creeds or dogmas—Individualism —The Supreme Power—Spiritual unfoldment—God's love and presence—All is One—What the idea of Oneness means—Man immortal —Assurance of immortality from the awakened spiritual consciousness—Theories not fundamental—Spiritual unfoldment—Thoughts are things—The attractive power of thought—Mind is positive to the body—Latent forces to be developed.

How often we hear this question: "What is the 'New Thought'?" And how difficult it is to answer such a question. The subject is so large, and the New Thought man or woman has grown into its truths so gradually that he or she finds it almost impossible to explain in a few words just what is meant by the term "New Thought." This is rendered particularly difficult by the fact that there are no creeds in the "New Thought". There are many cults and schools claiming allegiance to The New Thought, who differ very materially from each other in doctrine and details, but there are certain underlying principles to which all give adherence, though stating these principles in different ways, and using apparently contradictory terms. To answer the question which forms the title of this chapter, is no easy task, but let us see what we can do with it.

In the first place, The New Thought is the *oldest* thought in existence. It has been cherished by the chosen few in all ages, the masses of the people not having been ready for its teachings. It has been called by all names—has appeared in all guises. Every religion has within it certain esoteric teachings, not grasped by the many, but understood by the few, which hidden teachings contain much that is now being taught as The New Thought. The New Thought contains certain hints at mighty truths which have nestled in the bosom of the esoteric teachings of all religions —in the philosophies of the past and present—in the temples of the Orient—in the schools of ancient Greece. It is to be found in the songs of the poets—in the writings of the mystics. The advanced science of this age touches it without recognizing it fully.

It is not a thing that can well be conveyed by words—it is not easily comprehended by purely intellectual processes—it must be *felt* and lived out by those who are ready for it—those for whom the time has come. It has been known to the few throughout all ages and climes. All races have known it. It has been handed down from teacher to pupil from the earliest days. It contains the Truth to which Edward Carpenter refers, when he sings:

"O, let not the flame die out! Cherished age after age in its dark caverns, in its holy temples cherished. Fed by pure ministers of love—let not the flame die out."

The flame has been tenderly cared for down the ages. Many lamps have been lighted at the shrine, and have carried away with them a tiny bit of the sacred fire. The few in all ages have kept the flame alight by adding the oil of the spirit—that which comes from the inmost recesses of the soul. To protect this flame many have suffered death—persecution—contumely—revilement—disgrace. Some have been compelled to assume an air of mystery and charlatanism in order to distract the attention of the masses, and thus keep sheltered this bit of sacred flame. Ancient writers have carefully placed bits of this esoteric truth among writings of wide circulation, knowing that only those with the key could read, and the multitude would not even suspect the existence of the grain of wheat among the chaff. The advanced New Thought man of today may pick up the writings of all ages, and will see deep truths therein set forth in language perfectly clear to him, but which means nothing but words to the ordinary reader. The sacred books of all religions may be read by one who has the key, and the Greek philosophers, from Plato down, take on another meaning when one understands the principles underlying the esoteric teachings. And the modern writers also may be read with new insight, when one has grown into touch with the underlying principles. Shakespeare, Bacon, Pope, Browning, Emerson, Whitman and Carpenter, have many dark corners and hard sayings which are illuminated and made plain when one has obtained possession of the central thought—the Oneness of All.

Down, down through the ages has this Truth come to us, but it seems reserved for this age to have it spread broadcast among the people. And yet to many the message does not appeal. Some grasp a few scattering truths and think that they have it, but fail to see the real underlying principle of Oneness. Others reject it entirely, not being ready for it. Others who are ready for it, seem to grasp it instinctively as if they had always known it—they recognize their own, which has come to them.

The mere calling of the attention of some to the truth, seems to awaken the first glimmer of recognition in them; others find it necessary to reflect upon the idea and awaken to a recognition of the Truth more slowly. To others, the time is not yet ripe for the recognition of the great Truth, but the seed is planted and the plant and blossom will appear in time. That which seems like the veriest nonsense to them now, will be brought home to them as the very truth when the time comes. A desire has been created that will cause a mental unrest until more light is received. As old Walt Whitman has said: "My words will itch in your ears till you understand them." And as the great American transcendentalist, Emerson, says: "You cannot escape from your good." These people who do not yet understand will carry the thought with them, which, like the lotus, will unfold naturally and gradually. The Truth once recognized cannot be lost. There is no standing still in Nature.

It is difficult to convey a hint of this Truth to any but those who are prepared to receive. To others it often seems like arrant folly. Emerson has well said: "Every man's words, who speaks from that life, must sound vain to those who do not dwell in the same thoughts on their own part. I dare not speak for it. My words do not carry its august sense; they fall short and cold. Only itself can inspire whom it will. * * * * * * Yet I desire by profane words, if sacred I may not use, to indicate the heaven of this deity, and to report what hints I have collected of the transcendant simplicity and energy of the Highest Law."

"WHAT IS THE NEW THOUGHT?" Let us see. In the first place it is a name by which is best known that great wave of spiritual and psychic thought that is passing over the world, sweeping away antiquated dogmas, creeds, materialism, bigotry, superstition, unfaith, intolerance, persecution, selfishness, fear, hate, intellectual tyranny and despotism, prejudice, narrowness, disease and perhaps even death. It is the wave that is bringing us liberty, freedom, self-help, brotherly love, fearlessness, courage, confidence, tolerance, advancement, development of latent powers, success, health and life.

It stands for all that makes for Man's Betterment—Freedom—Independence—Success—Health—Happiness. It carries the banner of Tolerance—Broadness—Brotherhood—Love—Charity and Self-Help. It teaches Man to stand upon his own feet—to work out his own salvation—to develop the powers latent within him—to assert his real Manhood—to be Strong, Merciful and Kind. It preaches the doctrine of "I Can and I Will"—the gospel of "I Do." It calls upon Man to cease his lamenting and repining, and urges him to stand erect and assert his right to live and be happy. It teaches him to be brave, as there is nothing to fear. It teaches

him to abolish Fearthought and Worry, and the other foul brood
of negative thoughts, such as Hate, Jealousy, Malice, Envy and
Uncharitableness, that have been keeping him in the mire of Despair and Failure. It teaches him these things, and much more.
The New Thought stands for the doctrine of The Fatherhood of
God—the Oneness of All—the Brotherhood of Man—the King-
ship of Self.

The New Thought has no creeds or dogmas. It is composed
of Individualists, each reserving the right to look at things with
his own eyes—to see the Truth as it presents itself to him—to
interpret that Truth by the light of his own reason, intuition and
spiritual discernment, and to let it manifest and express itself
through him in its own manner. Such a man cares nothing for
institutions—he finds *within* that which he seeks. He does his
own thinking, and recognizes no man or woman as an authorized
interpreter of that which can only be interpreted by one's own
soul. New Thought people differ very materially from each
other on minor points, words and manner of expression, but un-
derneath it all they understand one another, and a close analysis
shows that they are all standing firmly upon the sound rock of
Fundamental Truth. They all have a bit of the Truth, but no
one of them has all of the Truth. Each is working to the Centre
in his own way—along his own path. And yet, seen from above,
each is found to be walking along the Great Path toward the same
Goal.

I will try to give you a hasty glance at what I conceive to be
the fundamental principles underlying that which is called The
New Thought, without considering the side-issues affected by
many of us. My explanation must, of necessity, be crude and
imperfect, but I will do the best I can to make at least a partially
clear statement of the fundamental principle of The New
Thought.

In the first place The New Thought teaches that there is a
Supreme Power back of, underlying, and *in* all things. This
Supreme Power is Infinite, Illimitable, Eternal and Unchange-
able. It IS, has always been, and always will be. It is Omnipresent (present everywhere) ; Omnipotent (all powerful, possessing all the power that is) ; and Omniscient (all-knowing, all-
seeing, knowing everything, seeing everything). This Supreme
Power—Universal Presence—All Mind—may be called MIND,
SPIRIT, LAW, THE ABSOLUTE, FIRST CAUSE, NA-
TURE, UNIVERSAL PRINCIPLE, LIFE, or whatever name
best suits the taste of the person using the term, but call it what
you will you mean this Supreme Power—the Centre. Personally I prefer the word GOD, and have therefore used it in this
book, but when I say GOD I mean this great Universal Presence,

and not the conception of a limited God held by any man. I am
nc satisfied with any conception of GOD which limits him in the
slightest. To me GOD must be illimitable, and all of the Universe must be an emanation of him. I cannot accept any partial
idea of GOD—to me GOD must be the ALL. And I think that
a careful inquiry will reveal the fact that this is a fundamental
principle underlying The New Thought, remembering, always
that words count for nothing and ideas for everything, and that
the man or woman who claims to have outgrown "God," and
talks of Nature, Life, Law, or what not, means his or her conception of that which my inner consciousness tells me IS, and
which I mean when I say "GOD."

The New Thought holds that Man is unfolding in consciousness, and that many have now reached that stage of spiritual consciousness whereby they become *conscious* of the existence and
immanence of GOD, and thus *know* rather than entertain a belief
based upon the authority, real or assumed, of other men. This
God-consciousness to which the race is rapidly tending, is the
result of the unfoldment, development, and evolution of Man for
ages, and, when fully possessed by the race, will completely revo-
lutionize our present conceptions of life, our ethics, customs, conditions and economics.

The New Thought teaches that GOD is not a being afar off
from us, full of wrath and punishment, but that he is right here
with us; all around us, yes, even *in* us; understanding us from
the beginning; realizing our limitations; full of love; and pa-
tiently seeing the gradual growth and unfoldment which brings
us into a clearer understanding of him. The New Thought does
not know of the wrath of GOD—any such conception is cast into
the shadow by the dazzling, overpowering sight of GOD'S love.
As to the reason of GOD'S plans and laws, The New Thought
does not pretend to have knowledge, holding that this cannot be
known by Man in his present stage of development, although by
reason and intuition he is beginning to understand that all is
Good, and to see evidences of a loving, good, perfect, just and
wise plan, in all the experiences of life. And having that Intelligent Faith which comes of the God-consciousness, it rests content, saying "GOD *IS*—and all is well."

The New Thought teaches that All is One—that all the Universe, high and low, developed and undeveloped, manifest and
unmanifest, is One—all is an emanation of GOD. This brings
with it the corollary that everything in the universe is in touch
with every other thing, and all is in connection with the Centre—
GOD. It holds, with modern science, that every atom is a part of
a mighty whole, and that nothing can happen to any atom without a corresponding effect upon every other part of the whole. It

holds that the sense of separateness is an illusion of the undeveloped consciousness, but an illusion necessary in certain stages for the working out of the plan, or as a recent writer has said, "the sense of separateness is a working fiction of the Universe." When man has so far progressed in spiritual growth and unfoldment that certain heretofore dormant faculties awaken to consciousness, or rather, when man's consciousness has so far developed that it takes cognizance of certain faculties the existence of which has heretofore been unknown to it, that man becomes conscious of the Oneness of All, and his relation to all that is. It is not merely a matter of intellectual conception, it is the growth of a new consciousness. The man who possesses this, simply *knows;* the man who has it not, deems the idea allied to insanity. This Cosmic Knowing comes to many as an illumination; to others it is a matter of gradual and slow development.

This idea of the Oneness of All explains many problems that Man has considered incapable of solution. It is at the heart of all occult and esoteric teachings. It is at the centre of all religious thought, although it is hidden until one finds the key. It is the Key that opens all doors. It explains all contradictions—all paradoxes. It welds together all discrepancies—all opposing theories —all the different views of any subject. All is One—nothing can be left out of that Oneness—all and everything is included. Man cannot escape his Oneness with All, try as he may. Separateness and selfishness are seen as merely the result of ignorance, from which man is slowly emerging. Every man is doing the best he can, in his particular stage of development. And every man is growing, slowly but surely. Sin is but ignorance of the truth. Selfishness and the sense of Separateness are at the bottom of all that we call "sin." And, under the Law, when we wilfully hurt another, it rebounds upon ourselves. Evil, selfish thoughts and acts react upon ourselves. We cannot hurt another without injuring ourselves. It is not necessary for GOD to punish us—we punish ourselves. When the race finally understands and is conscious of the Oneness of All—when it has a knowledge of the Law—when it has a *consciousness* of things as they are, then will Separateness and Selfishness drop away like a cast-off cloak, and that which we call sin and injustice can no longer exist for the race. When the Fatherhood of GOD, and the Brotherhood of Man, become realities in the consciousness of Man, instead of beautiful ideals fondly cherished but considered impractical and impossible of realization, then will Life be that which has been dreamt of through the ages. This Oneness of All is one of the fundamental truths of The New Thought, although many of its followers seem to have but a faint conception of what it really means, and are but slowly growing into an understanding of what it will mean for the world.

The New Thought teaches that Man is immortal. Its teachers differ in their theories as to just how and where he will live in the future, and of such speculations I do not purpose speaking at length. I will say this, however, that when Man obtains that wonderful assurance of immortality from his awakened spiritual faculties, he sees no need of worrying about the "how" and "where". He *knows* that he is and will be. He has within him such an abiding sense of existence, and deathlessness, that all of man's speculations seem like idle theories to him—useful in their place, of course, but of no vital importance to him. He knows that there are no limits to the possible manifestations of life—he knows that "infinity plus infinity" would not begin to express the possibilities before him, and he frets not. He learns to live in the NOW, for he knows that he is in Eternity right now, just as much as he ever will be, and he proceeds to Live. He is concerned with Life, not with Death, and he Lives. He has confidence in GOD and in the Divine Plan, and is content. He knows that if our entire solar system, and every other system the suns of which are visible to Man, were dissolved into their original elements, he would still exist, and would be still in the Universe. He knows that the Universe is large, and that he is a part of it—that he cannot be left out or banished from the Universe—that he is an important atom, and that his destruction would disarrange and destroy the whole. He knows that while the Universe lasts—*he* lasts. That if he is destroyed the Universe is destroyed. He know that GOD had use for him or he would not be here, and he knows that GOD makes no mistakes—changes not his mind—and destroys no soul that he has expressed. He says: I am a Son of GOD; what I shall be doth not yet appear; but come what will I am *still* a Son of GOD; what my future may be, concerns me not—it is not my business—I will place my hand in that of the Father and say "Lead Thou me on.".

This idea of the Immortality of the Soul—that Man is a Spiritual being, is also a fundamental principle of The New Thought, although its teachers have differing ideas regarding the methods and plans of the future life. To me, personally, I can see Life only as being on an ascending scale, rising from lower to higher, and then on to higher and higher and higher, until my spiritual vision fails me. I believe that in the Universe are beings much lower than us in the spiritual scale; and that there are also others much more advanced, much more highly developed than ourselves, very gods as compared with us, and that we are progressing along the Path until some day we will be where they are; and that others now much lower will some day be where we are now,

and so on. This is but my finite view of an infinite subject, and
I do not *know* these things as I *do* know the fundamental fact.
These particular views are not fundamental, being nothing more
than a dim perception, aided in certain ways from outside sources,
so do not accept them unless you feel that they mean truth to you
—form your own concept, if you prefer. It will not make any
difference to the fundamental principle. If you have the consciousness of the fundamental principle of immortality, then theories and views and concepts are as nothing. Do not be satisfied
with theories—mine or anyone else's—there is no satisfaction until
your feet are firmly planted on the rock. Then, when you feel
the solid rock beneath you, you may amuse and instruct yourself
by playing at building houses, which you may tear down tomorrow to erect others more in accordance with your advanced ideals.
But the rock is there all the time, and you are on it.

The New Thought teaches us that there is a spiritual evolution
going on in Man—that he is growing, developing and unfolding
in spiritual attainment. That his mind is developing and causing
to unfold new faculties which will lead him to higher paths of attainment. That the Higher Reason is beginning to make itself
manifest. It teaches that the race is nearing the plane of Cosmic
Knowing. Teachers speak this Truth in different ways—using
different words—but the thing itself is a fundamental principle of
The New Thought.

The New Thought teaches also that "thoughts are things"—
that every thought we think goes forth, carrying with it force
which affects others to a greater or less extent, depending upon
the force behind our thought, and the mental attitude of the other
persons. And it teaches that like attracts like in the world of
thought—that a man attracts to himself thoughts in harmony
with his own—people in harmony with his thoughts—yes, that
even things are influenced by thought in varying degrees. It
teaches that "as a man thinketh in his heart so is he," and that a
man may change, and often does change, his entire character and
nature by a change of thoughts, an adjustment of his mental attitude. It teaches that Fearthought and Worry and all the rest of
the foul brood of negative thoughts attract thoughts, people,
things, from the outside, and pull the man down to the level of
his thought-pictures. And on the contrary a man may, by right
thinking, raise himself from the mire, and surround himself with
people and things corresponding to his thoughts. And it teaches
that thoughts take form in action. And it teaches that the Mind
is positive to the Body, and that a man may become sick or well
—diseased or free from disease, according to his thoughts and
mental attitude. It teaches that the mind of Man contains latent
forces, lying dormant, awaiting the day of their unfoldment,

which may be developed and trained and used in a wondrous way. It teaches that Man is in his infancy regarding the proper use of his mental powers. These things and similar things, expressed in scores of forms, according to the views of the respective teachers, are fundamental principles of The New Thought.

I can do no more than merely mention these things now. In the succeeding chapters, I will try to go into each phase of the subject a little more fully, but it would take many volumes before I could feel that I had even penetrated beneath the surface of the subject. And then remember that I am only giving you my little bit of the Truth. Every other man or woman has his or her bit, so that my portion is merely as a grain of sand on the sea-shore.

The New Thought is not a "fad" as many have supposed, although many have made it the amusement. of an idle hour. It is no new religion as others have thought—it contains within it only that which may be found in all the great religions of the world, but generally so safely hidden that only those who looked carefully could find it. It is no new religion, but it will help to throw new light on every religion, or shade of religious thought. It has no churches or temples—it allows its followers to worship in the temples of their fathers, or, if they prefer, in the open field, on the ocean, in the forest, in their rooms, anywhere—everywhere, for they cannot escape from the Universe, and GOD is everywhere, and everyone is in constant touch with him, and may feel the pressure of his hand if they will but allow it—will hear the whisper of his voice if they will but listen to it.

The man or woman who awakens into a consciousness of the real principles underlying and making up that which we call The New Thought, will have found a peace which exceeds in comfort anything that has ever been known—will feel a joy beyond anything that has ever been dreamt of—will have acquired a knowledge exceeding all that has ever been deemed possible. Words cannot express this thing—it must be seen, felt, lived, to be realized.

This, my friends, is my answer to the question, "What is 'The New Thought'?" That it does not answer it, I am fully aware, but I also see that one cannot answer such a question in a few words—perhaps it could not be fully answered in as many volumes as I have used sentences. It is too great. It means something to every man or woman who is attracted to it—each takes from it that suited to his needs, and leaves the rest for others. And draw from it what we may, the supply is never diminished. And so, it seems, I have merely answered the question by telling of a little that The New Thought means to me —just a little. So

if it means something else to you—something more than I have
mentioned—something different from what I have stated—do not
blame me or yourself—we simply see that which we have drawn
from the spring in our little cup—the spring is still full and constantly flowing. Your cupful is as good as mine—mine as good
as yours—so let us not dispute about it—nor yet compare cupfuls.
Let us, instead, drink of the sparkling, life-giving fluid that has
been given us, and shout aloud that others who are thirsty and
are seeking the spring, may know that it is found. It is not
yours, nor mine—it is the property of All.

CHAPTER II.

"THOUGHTS ARE THINGS."

Thought waves—Vibrations—Telepathy—Thought-transference—We are
all affected by thought-waves—Public opinion the result of thought-
waves—An almost irresistible influence, unless understood—The
attractive power of thought—Like attracts like—The thought of a
community—Making one's self positive to the thoughts of others—
Thought auras surround every one, affecting others—Attracting and
repelling—Attracting the best thoughts from outside—The mind is a
magnet—How to protect yourself from being unduly affected by the
minds of others—Fix your keynote—The inner influence stronger
than the outer—How you may avail yourself of the world's unexpressed thought—Unexpressed thought seeks eagerly for expression
—How to attract it.

Every thought that we think starts in motion thought-waves,
or vibrations, which travel along with greater or lesser speed and
intensity, varying with the force of the original thought, and
which affect, more or less, people far removed from the persons
sending forth the thought. We are constantly sending forth
thought influence, and are constantly receiving thought waves
from others. I do not now refer to thoughts deliberately sent
out to the mind of another, or thoughts deliberately received by
one from the mind of another, according to the well-known, and
well established, laws of Telepathy, but to the equally real, but
far less understood, unconscious sending forth and receiving of
thoughts. which is going on in each of us all the time. Of course
these are all different manifestations of what we call Telepathy,
or thought-transference, but the term is generally used to desig-
nate the conscious sending and receiving of mental messages.

This power of thought-transference is being continually exer-
cised by all people, generally indirectly and unconsciously. Our
thoughts create vibrations which are sent forth in waves in all
directions, and affect more or less all persons with whose minds
they come in contact. We can see instances of this in every-day
life. Men are affected by the thoughts of others in business, on
the street, in the theatre, in church, and in fact everywhere.
Public opinion is largely formed by the thoughts of a number of
vigorous, positive thinkers, sent forth in thought-waves, rapidly
influencing the whole country, the thought-wave gaining force as
it progresses, being added to by the thought vibrations of everyone whom it affects. Great waves of popular feeling sweep over

the country carrying before them all except those who understand the laws of mental influence, and who have protected themselves against these outside impressions. The combined thought-waves of the majority of the people beat against the mind of the individual and exercise an almost irresistible influence.

There is one very important fact in this study of the power of thought vibrations, which every man or woman should constantly carry in mind. I refer to the fact that the law of "like attracts like" maintains in the thought-world, and that one attracts to himself the thoughts of others which correspond in kind with those held by himself. A man who Hates will attract to himself all the Hateful and Malicious thought-waves within a large radius, and these added thoughts act as fuel to the fire of his base feelings, and render him more Hateful and Hating than ever. One who thinks Love, and has outgrown the old negative thoughts of imperfect development, will not attract these negative thoughts to him. They will pass him by, hurrying on to some point of attraction in the minds of others who are thinking along the same lines. And the man who thinks Love will attract to himself all the Loving thoughts within his circle of influence. Men instinctively recognize this force when they gather in the same neighborhood with others in the same line of thought. Communities have their individualities just as persons do. Every village, town, and city has its own peculiarities, which are noticeable to those who enter it. And strangers moving into these communities gradually take on the characteristics of the place, unless the same prove very uncongenial to them, in which case they manage to move away from the town as soon as possible, and are not contented so long as they are within its borders. It is well to be surrounded by those whose thoughts are akin to our own, as we thus add to each other's power and are comparatively free from outside disturbing influences. Of course persons may by practice, and understanding, make themselves positive to the thoughts of others, and may with impunity allow themselves to be surrounded with persons of an entirely different line of thought, and may even, when so doing, attract to themselves, from greater distances, the thoughts which harmonize with their own.

Every person is constantly surrounded with a thought-aura which affects those with whom he comes in contact. Some people attract us without a word being spoken, while others repel us as soon as we come within the radius of their aura. The aura of a man is composed of the essence of his prevailing thoughts—it reflects his general mental attitude. This aura is felt not only by man, but also by the lower animals. Children are very susceptible to its influences, and many unaccountable likes and dislikes of children are explainable in no other way.

Some persons are very sensitive to the thought atmosphere of others, and will sense at once the mental attitude of those with whom they come in contact. Some psychics are able to perceive this aura, and state that it varies in density and shade according to the prevailing quality of thought of the individual.

When one realizes the wonderful workings of the law of thought-attraction he sees the importance of so controlling his thoughts that he may attract only the best and most helpful thought of the world, instead of the depressing, hurtful, negative thought which is being sent out from so many minds. A man who maintains a hopeful, confident, fearless mental attitude will attract to himself like thought from others, and will be strengthened and helped by the influx of the outside thought, and will go on from success to success, aided by the combined force of the thoughts which he has attracted to him. He becomes as a magnet drawing to himself that which strengthens and aids him. Equally true is the fact that the man who maintains a negative, fearful, despondent mental attitude will attract to himself like thoughts from the great field of thought, which will pull and drag him down still deeper into the Slough of Despond. Remember, always, "like attracts like" in the thought world. And you may rest assured that whatsoever you think will attract a corresponding thought which has been sent out from the minds of others.

Have you ever noticed the attractive power of thought in the cases of strangers brought into contact with each other? Each draws to himself his kind. Place a hundred strange men or women in a room, and inside of an hour they have formed themselves into groups, each group representing a different type—a different mental attitude. Each instinctively attracts and is attracted by corresponding qualities in another.

If you would develop along certain lines the best plan is to think along the desired lines as much as you can, endeavoring to hold the thoughts relating to it as much as possible. By doing so you will not only develop the mind by auto-suggestion, but will attract, from the great ocean of thought, the helpful thoughts which have been sent out by others, and you will obtain the benefit of their thinking, as well as your own. Many of us have been thinking along certain lines very intently and with full powers of concentration, and suddenly a bright idea will come into our minds from out of the Somewhere, and we will be almost startled at suddenly coming in possession of a valuable thought relating to the matter in hand. Vigorous, positive, hopeful, expectant, concentrated thought on almost any subject will bring to itself helpful and valuable thoughts from others. There is no question but that many men have developed powers in this direction that place them in touch with the best minds working along similar lines. Many inventors will find themselves pro-ducing the same invention, and writers frequently find that the book that they have just written bears a striking resemblance to one simultaneously produced by another writer in perhaps a different country. Much harsh feeling is often engendered by a lack of understanding of the workings of the law of thought.

I have spoken at considerable length upon this subject in my previous work, entitled "Thought Force," and can merely refer to it in the present volume. It, however, plays an important part in the teachings of The New Thought, and the student soon real-izes its wonderful bearing upon the affairs of everyday life.

There is no occasion for alarm on the part of any one because of the possibility of being unduly affected by the thoughts of others. The remedy is to place yourself in the proper key, that you may receive only the helpful vibrations corresponding to the thoughts uppermost in your own mind. Every man is master of his own mind, and nothing will enter there unless he permits it. The inside influence is much stronger than the outside. All one has to do is to keep his own mind free from base, negative thoughts and the undesirable thoughts of others will not be at-tracted to him. Only the thoughts that harmonize will find a congenial shelter within his mind. He fixes his own mental key-note and his mind will not respond to any other key. If he thinks Love, Hate will not come near him; if he thinks Truth, Lying thoughts will flee from him. "As a man thinketh in his heart, so is he," applies here also.

Man has wonderful possibilities in the direction of so devel-oping his mind that he may attract to himself that which he needs from the great world's store-house of unexpressed thought. He will find enormous quantities of unexpressed thought longing for expression, which will eagerly pour into his mind for that expression which was not given by the mind in which they orig-inated. Thoughts are hungry for expression, and flock to the mind of him who has sufficient energy to express the thoughts which come to him. Many men are too lazy to express the great thoughts which they originate, and it remains for others to absorb these unexpressed thoughts and use them. Noth-ing goes to waste, and what one man will not use another will be found to avail himself of. Unexpressed thought is added to the common store, to be drawn upon by all who need it and will attract it to themselves.

Your mind is a magnet drawing to it thoughts in keeping with your conscious or unconscious demands and desires. By cultivating the proper mental attitude you may draw the very best product of the world's thinking. Is it not worth trying?

CHAPTER III.

THE LAW OF ATTRACTION.

This Law difficult to understand—Thought attracts not only persons but things—Exerts a control over circumstances—The Oneness of All affords a solution to the problem—The atom attracts that which is needed for its development—The power of Desire—How the Law operates in some circumstances—The Law operating through men—Illustrations of the wonderful workings of the Law—Your thoughts place you in connection with the outer world and its forces—Starting the forces into operation—The road to Success—Swept on by irresistible forces—Faith and recognition of the Law, rewarded by immediate movement—One gets very much what he looks for—The Law is either your master or your servant.

The working of the Law of Attraction is something that puzzled me very much for a long time after I became interested in The New Thought, and I am of the opinion that others find it difficult to grasp. It is comparatively easy to understand the effect of the mind on the body—the mind on the minds of others—the will-power on the mind—the fact that a thought will attract a like thought, etc. But when one is first made aware that there is such a thing as a Law of Attraction whereby one attracts *things* to him—exerts a control over circumstances by reason of the character of his thoughts—he is apt to find it hard to grasp the fact, or to understand the Law which operates in this way. There is a great difference, apparently, between the effect of thought upon persons, and the effect of thoughts upon things. But when one grasps the idea of the Oneness of All, he will begin to understand why one part of the whole will affect another part of the whole, be that other part a person or a thing. I have never heard a complete, *clear* explanation of the inner working of the Law of Attraction, although many understand the general workings, and a fair idea may be obtained by reasoning by analogy. But that the Law of Attraction *exists*, and is in full working force, many men and women know by experience, and the beginner who cannot understand will find it necessary to take the Law on faith at the start, until he becomes convinced of its real existence, by the results obtained by himself.

There seems to be a great law of Nature whereby an atom attracts to itself that which is needed for its development. And the force that brings about these results manifests itself in Desire. There may be many Desires, but the predominant one has the strongest attracting power. This law is recognized through the various kingdoms of Nature, but it is only beginning to be realized that the same Law maintains in the kingdom of the mind.

Our mental attitude causes us to draw things to us corresponding in kind to our predominant thoughts and desires. A thought firmly fixed in the mind, and held continually, will attract to its holder the things represented by that thought, excepting in such cases where other mental influences are at work counteracting the power of the thought. For instance, if two men were to earnestly wish for the same thing, the stronger thought force would gain the object. But it is not always best to wish for some special thing, as that particular thing may not be the best thing for you in your present stage of development. The better plan is to hold the thought of ultimate success, leaving the details to the workings of the Law, and taking advantage of the things that occur, turning each one to your advantage, and allowing no chance to pass by without making use of it. It will be found that the Law operates that way. I have seen people who fixed their ambition and aspirations upon some particular thing, and after obtaining that thing would find out that it was not what they wanted at all. The better plan, as I have stated, is to hold to the mental attitude of success and accomplishment, leaving the details to be worked out from day to day—taking advantage of each feature of the plan as it presents itself, and feeling, always, that the particular thing that is occurring is the best possible thing that could happen, in view of ultimate success.

I believe that much of the work of the Law of Attraction is accomplished by means of one attracting to himself men of similar ideas, who are likely to be interested in his plans, ideas, business, etc., and at the same time causing one to be attracted to other men who may be of use to him. It is a case of mutual attraction, not a case of the influence of one mind over another. Two men of similar mental attitudes will attract each other and will come together for mutual advantage. And although the result often seems to be the attracting of *things,* it will be seen that the things are moved by men. Many other important results occur by one having attracted to himself thoughts and ideas from outside, which he puts into practice and thereby is enabled to realize his desire. But there are cases in which it is seen that the mind has a positive effect upon *things.* Some men seem to be immune from accidents, while others are always running into them. Men of a fearless, daring nature seem to be exempt from many things that occur to men who are full of fear. Some men seem to bear charmed lives in battle, while others are always being wounded. I have heard of a number of cases in which men have almost sought death, and could not find it. At first glance it would ap-

pear that the thing they sought should have come to them, but
a little closer analysis shows us that what they really did was
to get rid of fear.

And the same thing seems true of business and everyday life.
The man who dares and seems devoid of fear, takes all sorts of
chances but generally comes out ahead in the end. If he fails, it
is generally because he loses his nerve at the last moment. Fear
is one of the greatest attracting forces of the mind. It is equal
to Confident Expectation, in fact Fear is a sort of confident expectation of evil to come, the expectation varying in degree with
the amount of Fear.

Your thoughts place you in connection with the outside world
and its forces, and you attract and repel people, and things, by
the character of thought held. You and they are attracted to
each other, because your thoughts are pitched in the same key.
You are in close touch with all other parts of the whole, but attract to yourself only such of the parts as correspond in kind with
your mental attitude. If you think Success you will find that
you have started into operation the forces that are conducive to
that success, and from time to time, if you maintain the same
mental position, other things will fall into line as they are needed,
and will aid you in your efforts. Things will seem to come your
way in a most astonishing manner, and opportunities will arise
which, if taken advantage of, will insure to you success. You
will find that new thoughts will come into your mind which
should be taken advantage of. You will meet with people who
will help you in many ways, by suggestions, ideas and active
help. Of course the work which you must do yourself will not
be performed for you by others, but the Law will continually help
and assist you. It will bring opportunities and chances to your
door, but you will have to take them in. It will lead up to
doors opening into advancement, but you will have to open the
doors yourself. It will undertake what will seem to be round-about
roads to get to a thing, but do not let that worry you, for you
will arrive at your journey's end, no matter how winding the
road.

Sometimes it will take you away past the point at which you
thought you were aiming, and, as you go past, you will smile to
think how this point on the road which now seems so unimport-
ant, a little further back seemed to be your destination, your
reason for making the trip. Sometimes the thing which seems
to represent all that is worth having, and which inspires you
to make the effort, will have lost all interest for you when you
near it, and you will make no attempt to grasp it but pass on,
rapidly swept past by the irresistible forces which have been set
into operation.

Faith in the Law and recognition of it, seem to be rewarded by immediate movement forward. Lack of faith, and denial of it, seem to act as brakes to progress, although the law is always in operation, because if we are not going forward it is pulling us in some other direction, by reason of the forces of attraction which we have put into operation, even though we do it unconsciously. The Law works two ways, apparently, although both ways are really only different manifestations of the one. The thing you Fear attracts as much as the thing for which you hope.

When one is looking for trouble he generally gets it, and when he feels his ability to stand all sorts of trouble and to ride over it, the trouble does not seem to come. One gets very much what he looks for. The old saying that the world takes a man at his own valuation, although not strictly correct, is based upon a recognition of this Law. A man who expects to be kicked and buffeted around, generally has his expectations realized, whereas a man who demands respect generally gets it.

As I have already said, the Law will not do a man's work for him, but it places tools and materials right at his hand, and keeps him well supplied with both. The Law is constantly bringing opportunities to each of us, and it remains for us to take advantage of them or to let them pass us by unheeded. Thoughts, things, people, ideas, opportunities, chances, and other things which we attract are passing before us all the time. But it takes Courage to grasp them. The successful man is he who knows how to take advantage of the chances that other men fail to see. He has confidence in himself and in his ability to beat into shape the crude material at his hand. And so, he never feels that there are no more chances in the world for him, or that all the good things have been passed around. He knows that there are plenty more good things where the others came from, and he simply keeps his eyes open, and after a bit something comes along and he reaches out and takes it.

The Law of Attraction is in full operation. You are making use of it constantly and unconsciously, every minute of your life. What kind of things are you attracting to you? What kind of things do you want? Do your thoughts correspond with the things you want or the things you fear? Which? The Law is either your Master or your Servant. Make your choice, and make it NOW.

CHAPTER IV.

MIND BUILDING.

Advanced Man has the power of consciously building his mind—Doing the building yourself instead of letting others do it—The sub-conscious warehouse—Moving along the lines of least resistance—Taking mental stock and discarding worthless material—Worthless mental bric-a-brac—Man not a worm of the dust—Man's destiny great and glorious—Man's mind just what he makes it—Training and developing the mind—How to acquire desired mental traits—Moulding and shaping the mind according to the will—We are no longer servants of our minds—Mental freedom—The mind an instrument to be used by the Real Self—Auto-suggestions and affirmations—The doctrine of "I Can and I Will"—What kind of mental material are you using?

To the advanced Man is reserved the proud privilege of *consciously* building up his mind into any desired shape—the privilege of altering, repairing, and adding to the mental structure. In the lower animals, primitive man, and even the majority of men to-day, the work of building up the mind is largely performed by forces outside of himself—environment, associations, suggestions, etc., and, of course, even the most advanced man is subject to these influences. But the developed man knows that HE, himself, has a hand in the building up of his mind. This building, of course, is done altogether in the sub-conscious field, the conscious thought supplying the material, and the "I" being the builder. In a previous chapter, I have spoken of the Sub-conscious Plane of the mind, and how it is being added to, each day, by thoughts of the conscious plane of our own mind, the thoughts of others, suggestions, and so on. I have also compared the sub-conscious plane of mentation to a body of water into which a clear stream was flowing, and showed how the character of the entire body of water depended upon the quality of the water that was pouring in.

The sub-conscious mind may also be compared to an immense warehouse, into which goods are being carried and stored. It will readily be seen that the character of the contents of the warehouse must be determined by the grade and quality of the goods being carried in from day to day. This being granted, it will readily be seen how important becomes the selection of these mental goods which are being stored away.

The sub-conscious plane of the mind is an immense storehouse into which we are continually carrying goods to be stored

away for future use. And, moreover, these goods are being
constantly used. The greater part of our thinking is done along
the lines of sub-conscious mentation, and the sub-conscious plane
of the mind can only use that which has already been stored away
in its space.

Mind moves along the lines of least resistance, and when it
becomes necessary for us to think upon a certain subject, we
find ourselves taking the easiest line of thought, which is always
the line which has been traveled most frequently in the past.
It tires us to think along new lines, while to think upon the old
accustomed lines requires but little effort, and we consequently
move along the lines of least resistance. We have in our sub-
conscious plane of mind many cut-and-dried opinions, many
ready made ideas, upon which we have never seriously thought.
Sometime, in the past, we have accepted these opinions or ideas
from some source, and we have never seriously considered the
other side of the question. And yet when any of these subjects
come up in conversation, or reading, we find that we have well-
settled opinions upon them and are often quite bigoted regarding
them. It is only when we are forced to take out the old opinion
and idea and examine it carefully and closely, look it over, that
we find that there is no merit at all in it, and we are annoyed to
think that we have been keeping the old thing around the place
so long, and we discard it and replace it with a good sound
thought of our own manufacture. A good mental house-cleaning
will reveal to us many such useless and imperfect articles
around the sub-conscious storeroom.

Among the many worthless articles of mental *bric-a-brac* to
be found in most minds may be seen the thoughts of Fear, Worry,
Jealousy, Hate, Malice, Envy, etc. A careful examination of
these articles will result in their being thrown on the mental
waste-heap and suitable, up-to-date articles put in their places.
None of these articles will stand the tests of the Higher Reason.
And then the belief of man being a worm of the dust; a miserable
sinner worthy only of eternal damnation; a child of darkness
fit only for the fiery pit; all these beliefs have been passed on to
men and women, and they have stored them away in the sub-conscious storehouse and make use of them constantly.

How can any man believe himself to be a worm of the dust
and a child of darkness, and at the same time realize that he is
a Son of God with a destiny so great, so grand, and so brilliant,
that his mind cannot even conceive it? How can a man, with
such ideas ruling him, throw off the sheaths which he has outgrown, and step forward into a brighter spiritual consciousness?

And then the idea of Failure, Fear, Worry and the rest. Man
has had these things poured into him until he is so full of them

that they influence all his actions and thoughts. And the more he thinks and acts along these lines the more likely he is to continue such thoughts and actions in the future. He is traveling over and over the old road until it becomes second nature to do it and harder to strike out into a new path.

Man should realize that he is what he thinks. He should know that he is building up his mind, unconsciously it is true, by the character of the thoughts he is thinking. If he is thinking bright, cheerful, happy, confident and courageous thoughts, he is building up a mentality colored with these thoughts. And equally true is it that if he is thinking thoughts of fear, worry, gloom and despair, his mentality will take on that color, and all his actions will be influenced by the prevailing shade of his mental attitude.

In my previous work, entitled "Thought Force," I give a long chapter on "Character Building by Mental Control," which shows how a man can practically make himself over by cultivating a certain line of thought and letting it find lodgment in his subconscious mentality. One can, by continually keeping the mind in certain channels, so train and develop the faculties that they will soon take up the new habit of thought and will, without effort, follow the new mental path that has been mapped out for them. Remember, each time you think a thought, or act out a thought, you make it that much easier for your mind to do the same thing over again.

If you wish to be Energetic and Active, think as many energetic and active thoughts as you can and endeavor to act them out. Let your thoughts be constantly upon these subjects and endeavor to manifest the thought in action as much as possible. By following this course you will gradually make yourself over, so far as those habits are concerned, and the new way will be the natural way, and the old discarded habits will seem very unreal to you. One can train his mind in any direction desired, or considered needful. Remember, it is the conscious mentality training and shaping the sub-conscious. You are filling the sub-conscious storehouse with the goods you wish to use, and when you have occasion to bring out any of these mental goods you may expect to find only those which you have placed there.

The sub-conscious mentality may be trained just as one would train a child or pet animal. It may be moulded and shaped according to the will. It requires perseverance, of course, but it is an important thing to accomplish.

We have been servants of our minds for so long that we have grown to consider that state of affairs beyond remedy, and, although we do not like it, we have about resigned ourselves to the inevitable. The New Thought carries the message of mental

freedom to Man. It shows him that the mind is but a tool of the
Real Self—an instrument to be used—a machine that can be
taught to do his bidding. If the Desire is in a man he can mould
his mind to carry out his desires and aspirations.

If a man lacks certain qualities, he may develop and grow
these desirable qualities by constantly carrying them in mind and
manifesting them in action as often as may be. And if one wishes
to overcome certain weak thoughts and tendencies he may do so
by holding the thought exactly opposite to the one he wishes to
overcome. HE is in control if he will only assert himself. He
is master of the warehouse and has the power to admit only such
goods as he considers desirable.

Auto-suggestions and affirmations are practically the same.
They consist of certain statements, which, constantly repeated or
affirmed by one, will cause to grow within him the qualities corresponding to the auto-suggestion or affirmation.

If one lacks confidence in himself and is timid, bashful or
faint-hearted, the affirmation, "I CAN AND I WILL," will prove
a wonderful mental tonic. Let him repeat it over and over again,
not like a parrot, but with a full conception of its meaning, and
before long he will find the "I Can and I Will" vibrations beginning to manifest themselves in him. And when he is suddenly confronted with a proposition, or task, he will find the thought,
"I Can and I Will," springing into being and the action following on its heels. Before this change he felt nothing but "I Can't"
and "I'm Afraid" when confronted with anything new. He
will have made himself over.

And so it is with any line of thought. Get into the habit of
thinking of yourself as you wish yourself to be, and before long
you will find yourself growing into just that thing.

You are building up your mind constantly—you are erecting
the edifice of character every day. How are you building it—
what materials are you using in the edifice? Are you using the
best material possible—the positive, bright, confident thought
materials? Or are you using the defective, imperfect, negative,
fearful materials that so many have used?

While you are building up your mind, why don't you do it
right? Why don't you insist upon nothing but the best material
being used and reject all of the undesirable kind? You have
the operation in hand—you are the builder. If you make a poor
job of it, don't blame anyone but yourself. You are building to-
day—*what kind of material are you using?*

CHAPTER V.

THE DWELLER OF THE THRESHOLD.

Bulwer Lytton's creation—The frightful monster confronting the neophyte in the secret chamber—The real meaning of the occult figure of speech—Fear the great obstacle to success and happiness, and spiritual attainment—Stands at the door to Freedom—Keeps the race in bondage—No advancement possible until it is overcome—And it can be overcome—Confront it boldly and it retreats—Assert the I Am—Fear is as much a magnet as Desire—Fear the parent of all the brood of negative thought—Illustrations—Fear has hypnotized the race—Fear never did Man any good, and never will—The cry of "I'm afraid" has always been heard—Opposition to new ideas—How Fear may be defeated—Fear a humbug and a bugaboo, without any real power over us except that which we allow him.

Many of you have read Edward Bulwer Lytton's occult story, "Zanoni," and remember the "Dweller of the Threshold," that frightful monster which confronted the neophyte, Glyndon, in the secret chamber of the master, Mejnour, and of which Mejnour speaks when he says: "Amidst the dwellers of the Threshold is One, too, surpassing in malignity and hatred all her tribe—one whose eyes have paralyzed the bravest and whose power increases over the spirit precisely in proportion to its fear."

In another chapter Glyndon seeks to penetrate the mysteries of the secret chamber and meets the hideous keeper of the door, which is described thus: "* * * The casement became darkened with some object undistinguishable at the first gaze, but which sufficed mysteriously to change into ineffable horror the delight he had before experienced. By degrees this object shaped itself to his sight. It was that of a human head, covered with a dark veil, through which glared with livid and demoniac fire eyes that froze the marrow of his bones. Nothing else of the face was distinguishable—nothing but those intolerable eyes. * * * It seemed rather to crawl as some vast misshapen reptile; and, pausing at length, it cowered beside the table which held the mystic volume and again fixed its eyes through the filmy veil on the rash invoker. * * * Clinging with the grasp of agony to the wall, his hair erect, his eye-balls starting, he still gazed back upon that appalling gaze. The Image spoke to him—his soul rather than his ear comprehended the words it said: 'Thou hast entered the immeasurable region. I am the Dweller of the Threshold'."

Those familiar with occult symbols and figures recognize in
Lytton's Dweller of the Threshold that enemy of Man's progress—that frightful figure that stands before the door to freedom—FEAR.

Fear is the first and great enemy to be overcome by the man
or woman who wishes to escape from bondage and attain Freedom. The door to Freedom is pointed out and the seeker makes
a few steps in that direction, but is halted by the sight of the
malignant Dweller of the Threshold—FEAR. Lytton has not
painted it in too frightful form—words cannot describe the
hideousness of this monster.

Fear stands in the road of all progress—all advancement—
escape. Fear is at the bottom of all of Man's failures—sorrows—
unhappinesses. The Fear of the race keeps it in bondage—the
Fear of the individual keeps him a slave. Until Fear is overcome there can be no advancement for either individual or race.
This enemy must be overcome before there can be escape. And
it *can* be overcome by those who will face it calmly and boldly.
Look Fear square in the eyes and her eyes drop and she retreats
before you. Assert the I AM, and know, in the depths of your
soul, that nothing can injure the real "I," and Fear flies before
you, fearing that you will conquer her and bind her with chains—
she knows the power of the I AM consciousness.

When a man allows Fear to enter his heart he attracts to him
all that which he fears. Fear is a powerful magnet and exer-
cises a wonderful attracting power. Besides this it paralyzes
the efforts and energy of the man and prevents him from doing
that which he could easily do were he free of the monster. Man
succeeds in proportion as he frees himself from Fear. Show me
the successful man and I will show you a man who has *dared* and
who has turned his back upon Fear.

Take your own life, for instance. You have had many opportunities offered you which you have allowed to pass you because of Fear. You have met with a fair degree of success, and,
at the last moment, when the prize was in sight, you have drawn
back your hand and fled to the rear. Why? Because you "lost
your nerve" and Fear entered your heart. When the microbe
of Fear enters the system the entire body is paralyzed.

Fear is the parent of the entire brood of negative thoughts
which keep men in bondage. From her womb spring Worry,
Jealousy, Hate, Malice, Envy, Uncharitableness, Bigotry, Intolerance, Condemnation, Anger and the rest of the foul brood. You
doubt this, do you? Well, let us see. You do not worry about
things unless you fear them; you do not feel jealous unless fear
is also present; hate is always mingled with fear and springs
from it—one does not hate a thing that is beyond the power of

hurting him; envy shows its origin; bigotry, intolerance and condemnation all arise from fear—persecution begins only when the object is feared; a close analysis will show that anger springs from a vague sense of fear of the thing which causes the anger— a thing that is not feared causes amusement and derision rather than anger. Analyze closely and you will find that all of these negative, hurtful thoughts bear a close family resemblance to their parent—Fear. And if you will start in to work and will abolish Fear the foul brood of youngsters will die for want of nourishment.

Fear has hypnotized the race for ages, and its effects are as noticeable now as ever. We have taken in Fear with our mother's milk—yes, even before birth we have been cursed with this thing. We have had it suggested into us from childhood. The "ifs," "supposings," "buts," "what-ifs" and "aren't-you-afraids" have always been with us. We have been taught to fear everything in the heavens above, the earth beneath and the waters under the earth. The bugaboos of childhood—the things-to-be-feared of manhood—are all off the same piece. We are told all our lives that "the goblins will catch you if you don't look out." Turn which way we may the suggestions of Fear are constantly being poured into us. Any one who knows the power of repeated suggestions can realize what all this has meant to the world. The brave band of New Thought people—Don't Worry people—and others of this line of thought, are doing much toward pouring a stream of clear, living water into the muddy, stagnant pool of Fearthought that the world has allowed to accumulate, and others are adding to the stream every day, but the pool is enormous.

Fear never accomplished any good and never will. It is a negative thought which has dragged its slimy form along the ages, seeking to devour all which promised good to Mankind. It is the greatest enemy of progress—the sworn foe of Freedom. The cry, "I'm afraid," has always been heard, and it is only when some man or woman, or a number of them, has dared to laugh in its face, that some bold deed has been done that has caused the world to go forward a notch or so. Let some one advance a new idea calculated to benefit the world, and at once you hear the cry of Fear, with the accompanying yells of the whelps, Hate and Anger, filling the air and awakening echoing yells, growls and snarls from all the Fear-kennels within hearing distance. Let any one try to do a thing in a new way—improve upon some accepted plan—teach the Truth in a new way—and the yell goes up. Fear is the curse of the race.

The man who is in bondage to Fear is a very slave, and no crueler master ever existed. In proportion to his fear, Man

sinks in the mud. And the pathetic, although somewhat humor-
ous, part of it all is, that all the time the man has sufficient power
to rise up and smite his task-master a blow between the eyes
which will cause him to retreat in a hurry. Man is like a young
elephant which has not yet recognized its strength. When one
once realizes that nothing can hurt him, Fear flees from him.
The man who recognizes just what he is, and what is his place
in the Universe, parts company with Fear forever. And, before
he reaches this stage, Fear loses its hold upon him as he advances step by step toward that recognition.

And not only on this plane may Fear be defeated, but even
on the lower plane of self-interest and self-advancement Fear may
be gotten rid of. When Man recognizes that Fear is a sort of
home-made, pumpkin-headed jack-o'-lantern, instead of the fiery-
eyed monster of the night he had supposed it to be, he will walk
up to it and knock it off the fence post where it had been placed
to frighten him. He will see that the things that happen are never
so bad as the things that were feared. He will see that the Fear
of a thing is worse than the thing itself. He will see that, as the
anticipation of a desired thing is greater than the realization, so
is the anticipation of a feared thing worse than the happening
of it. And he will find that the majority of feared things do not
happen. And he will find that even when things do happen, somehow matters are straightened out so that we bear the burden
much better than we had dreamt would be possible—God not
only tempers the wind to the shorn lamb, but he tempers the shorn
lamb to the wind.

And Man finds that the very fearing of a thing often brings
it upon him while a fearless mental attitude sends the thing flying
away often at the last moment. Job cried out, "The thing that
I feared hath come upon me."

Some one has said, and I have often repeated it: "There is nothing to be feared but Fear." Well, I go further than that now
and say that there is no sense in fearing even Fear, for, as terrible as he appears on the outside, he is made of the flimsiest material on the inside. He is "a lath painted to resemble iron."
A few strong blows will smash him. He is a fraud—a yellow
dog wearing a lion's skin. Stand up before him and smile
boldly in his face—look him in the eyes and smile. Do not mind
his frightful form—his hideous mask—he is a weakling when
matched with Courage and Confidence. All these negative
thoughts are weaklings when compared with their opposites on
the positive plane.

Would you know how to get rid of Fear? Then listen. The
way to get rid of Fear is to ignore his existence and to carry before you, and with you always, the ideals of Courage and Confi-

dence. Confidence in the great plan of which you are a part. Courage in your strength as a part of the whole. Confidence in the workings of the Law. Courage in your ability to work in accordance with the Law. Confidence in your destiny. Courage in your knowledge of the reality of the Whole and the illusions of separateness. Courage and Confidence arising from the knowledge of the Law of Attraction and the power of Thought-force. Courage and Confidence in your knowledge that the Positive always overcomes the Negative.

Men often say that The New Thought principles are beyond them—that they cannot comprehend—that they want something that will be of use to them in their every day lives. Well, here is something for such people. This idea of the abolishing of Fear will make them over and will give them a peace of mind that they have never been conscious of before. It will give them sweet sleep after business hours; it will give them an even mind during business hours; it will make their paths smoother and will obviate friction: it will soon be used to cause things to "come their way." And while it is doing these things for them it will be making better men of them. It will be preparing them for the recognition of higher truths.

You neophyte, who are standing at the door of the secret chamber, longing to pass through its portals and thence to knowledge and freedom and power, be not dismayed at the sight of the Dweller of the Threshold. He is merely "gotten up for the occasion." Smile in his face and gaze steadily into his eyes and you will see what an old humbug he is. Push him aside and enter into the room of knowledge. Beyond that are other rooms for you, which you will pass through in turn. Leave the Dweller for timid mortals who are afraid that the "goblins will get them." Faint heart never won fair lady nor anything else worth having in this world. And "none but the brave deserve the fair," or anything else. So drop your whining cry of "I Can't" or your sniveling "I'm afraid," and, shouting boldly, "I CAN AND I WILL," brush past the Dweller of the Threshold, crowd him up against the door-post with your shoulder and walk into the Room.

CHAPTER VI.

MIND AND BODY.

Many persons attracted to the New Thought by the healing feature—This feature highly important but not the highest good obtainable—Many theories but only one real force—The secret of permanent cures— The claims of the different schools—All obtaining wonderful results —All forms of healing good, but cures can be made by one's self— The healing power latent in the individual—Called into force by outside treatment—The sub-conscious plane in healing—Absent treatment—Man has a latent recuperative power within him—Arouse the recuperative power—Vital force—Use of transference of Vital Force—Fear as a poison—Taking off the brake—No special mystery about healing—Explanation of Nature's processes in mental healing.

Many persons are under the impression that the healing of disease is the main object and underlying principle of The New Thought. And it is probable that the majority of persons who become interested in this great movement have been attracted, originally, by this particular feature. The person whose attention is attracted by this feature, however, soon sees the deeper phases of the thought and begins to investigate them and before long the mere healing of disease, as important as it is, sinks into comparative insignificance. Many begin by taking treatment from some practitioner of mental healing (or spiritual healing, as some prefer to term it) and then work into the higher phases, while some become interested in the higher truths, and find themselves becoming stronger physically, without any special effort on their part.

I do not purpose going into the theory of mental healing, or the influence of the mind upon the body, and can do no more than to merely touch upon the subject in a general way. There are many books treating fully upon this subject, and the majority of my readers know from personal experience of the success that has attended this method of the treatment of disease. Each particular school of mental healing seems to have its own pet theories, and manner of giving treatments. Some prefer personal treatments, others prefer what are called "absent treatments," wherein the person giving the treatment may be many miles from the patient, the healing thought being communicated telepathically. Personally, I believe that all these different forms of treatment are but different forms of calling into operation the same force—the wonderful power of the mind over the body.

I believe that the best plan of treatment is to educate the patient to recognize the wonderful powers of his own mind in healing himself, and I also believe that no *permanent* cure is effected, and future disease prevented, until the patient grows into a recognition of this fact. But, as one must crawl before he can walk, so is it often necessary for the patient, grown weak in body and mind, and distrustful of his own powers, to receive assistance in the shape of some form of treatment from outside.

We hear a great deal of the claims of the several schools and cults, each of which seems to think that its way is the only way, and that all other methods are erroneous, or, at least, not quite the real thing. Some of this reasoning is very plausible and convincing, until we look around and see that all the schools and cults are obtaining great results, and a little closer investigation will show that the percentage of cures is about the same in each case, notwithstanding the claims of each particular school or set of practitioners. I know that they *all* obtain results, but, as I have already said, I believe that the best permanent results are obtained by those practitioners who, while giving treatments, gradually educate their patients to help themselves and to stand upon their own feet, and assert their God-given power to manifest health.

I believe that the several practitioners of Christian Science, Mental Science, Suggestive Therapeutics, Faith Cure, Divine Science, and all the rest, are using the same great force, the only difference being in the method of application. And I know also, from personal experience, that it is quite possible for a man to realize the healing power within himself. and by applying same to bring about a complete restoration of health and energy without the assistance of any one else.

I believe that the healing power is latent within the individual, and that, when he is treated and cured by another, the cure has been effected by the practitioner calling into life and activity that healing power. This awakening of the power within may be accomplished by any of the various methods of personal treatment or by absent treatment. In the latter case the positive thought-waves of the practitioner beat upon the mind of the patient (on the sub-conscious plane) and awaken the latent force therein, and the cure results. The effect of the mind of the practitioner, whether conveyed by verbal suggestion or telepathy, acts just as does the powerful and repeated auto-suggestion, or affirmation, of the patient himself. Both reach the sub-conscious plane of the patient and restore the normal condition of that portion of the mind having charge of the physical functions. And the mind, thus restored to normal action, sends the proper impulses over the sympathetic nervous system to the affected parts, supplying such parts with an increased nerve-current and circulation of the blood, thus repairing the worn-out and broken-down tissue and cells and causing the organ to function properly.

In other words, I believe that the real work is done through the mind of the patient—through the healing power called into force in one of several ways and working through the brain, or brains, and nervous system of the patient. Every man or woman has within him, or her, dormant in many cases and inactive in many others, a certain recuperative power capable of restoring lost function and strength to diseased organs and parts. This power may be aroused by the mental effort of the practitioner, his suggestions, treatments, ceremonies, remedies, etc., and also by the will power or faith within the patient himself. But it is the same force awakened in all cases and the same power that does the healing work. I, of course, recognize that it is possible for one person to transfer what has been called "vital force" from his organism to that of a weakened patient, but this vitality so transferred is but in the nature of a "tonic," and merely adds strength to the patient to carry him along until the mental forces do their work. In the case of a patient very much weakened it is impossible for the mind to send correct impulses to the body, because the brain has become weakened by the waste of power, and it becomes necessary for the patient to avail himself of the assistance afforded by the practitioner's highly developed vitality, until he regains enough strength to carry on the work himself.

In many cases of sickness, particularly in cases of functional disorders, the recuperative force of the patient is neutralized by the mind of the patient being full of Fear thoughts, which act as a cause of disease in many cases, and also prevent the patient from using his own recuperative force given him by Nature for that purpose. Fear is a poison that has killed millions, and Worry is its oldest child, who is striving hard to reach the record established by its parent.

I have always held, in spite of the opposition of other writers, that a large percentage of the cures effected by New Thought healing has been accomplished, not by the doing of any special thing toward a cure, but simply by inducing the patient to refrain from worrying and fearing and harboring negative thoughts. When the patient "takes off the brake" that he has imposed upon his own recuperative mental forces, these forces start in at once to do their work and a cure ensues. It is on the same principle that it is not necessary for one to take a shovel and start to work to shovel out the darkness from a room—all that is necessary is to open the windows and "let a little sunshine in." When the windows are opened and Hope and Courage are allowed to flow in, Fear, Worry and the rest of the monsters of the darkness flee, and the sunny thoughts soon destroy the microbes that have been infesting the mental room.

There is no special mystery about the way New Thought cures are effected. Nothing miraculous or astonishing, when one learns something about Nature's processes. When the recuperative forces are aroused, or when the brake of Wrong Thinking has been raised, Nature proceeds to send an increased nerve current to the affected part. This work is done along sub-conscious lines, over the great nerve centers and sympathetic nervous system. This nerve current is like a current of electricity being sent to the parts from that great dynamo—the Brain. This nerve current vitalizes the organ or part, and also causes an increased circulation of the blood to the part. Nature builds up bodies by means of the blood, which, flowing through the arteries, carries liquid flesh and nourishment to every part of the body—to every organ and part—building, repairing, replenishing, restoring, replacing and nourishing. The blood on its return journey to the heart, through the veins, carries with it the broken-down tissue, waste-products and other garbage of the system, which is burned up and destroyed by the oxygen taken in the lungs and to which the blood is exposed on its return journey. No part of the body—no organ—can be properly nourished and stimulated unless it has a normal nerve-current and a proper supply of blood. And when a man's mind is filled with negative, worrying, fearful thoughts, or thoughts of Hate, Malice or Jealousy, it is impossible for him to send the proper nerve-current to the parts of his body, and, the circulation becoming affected, he begins to manifest what we call Disease. When normal conditions of the mind are restored normal conditions of the body follow.

The action of the heart is increased by certain emotions; the cheek flushes or pales from certain thoughts, the digestion is impaired by certain thoughts; and so on. And the same thing is manifested on a larger scale when improper thinking becomes a habit. Improper thinking results in improper living—the two go hand in hand. Show me what a man thinks and I will show you what he does and how he lives, and what is the state of his health. I have not space to tell you just how each particular thought affects one, but I can safely say that that miserable thought FEAR is the parent of the entire brood of negative thoughts, and if you get rid of him, you will exterminate the whole brood, as he not only begets but also nourishes each of his offspring. Abolish him at once.

CHAPTER VII.

THE MIND AND ITS PLANES.

The theory of the duality of the mind, and its weak points—Man has but
one mind, but it functions upon two planes—The Conscious and the
Sub-conscious—The Sub-conscious not the soul, but merely one
field of mentation—Super-conscious faculties really the source of
higher knowledge—Conscious thought is fresh from the mint—Sub-
conscious thought is the results of preceding conscious thought of
self or others—Thought impulses and habits—Conscious thoughts
meet new condition—Sub-conscious thoughts handle familiar problems—Man exhibits the highest form of Conscious mentation—
Human sheep—The mind and the Will—The secret of the Oriental
occultists—Evolutionary development still progressing.

Many modern writers have endeavored to explain the apparent duality of the mind of Man, by erecting elaborate, theoretical
edifices upon the firm foundation of the dual functioning of the
mind. Some of these writers have carried their reasoning to absurd lengths, and have attempted to explain all of the problems
of existence by their theories of the duality of the mind. They
have assumed that because Man has a mind capable of functioning along two different lines of effort, he must, necessarily, have
two minds. Some have styled these two minds, respectively, the
Objective and Subjective. Others have preferred the terms Conscious and Sub-conscious. Still others, have thought that the
terms Voluntary and Involuntary best conveyed the idea. But all
have assumed that Man had two distinct minds—some even considering them as separate entities. They ignored the fact that it
was almost impossible to separate the two minds; they failed to
state that the qualities attributed to the two respective minds
seemed to shade into each other. They failed to tell us just where
the Objective left off and the Subjective began. These theories
have proved very useful as working hypotheses, enabling us to
work into better things, but as permanent solutions of the problems of the mind, they have failed of their purpose, and while
tyros in the New Psychology have accepted them eagerly as af-
fording a solution of the entire question, those who have gone
deeper into the subject have found it necessary to regard such
theories as but imperfect working hypotheses, at the best.

The idea that Man has two minds, is today regarded as only a
working-fiction by many of the most careful investigators of the
subject. They realize that man has but one mind, functioning

along two different planes of effort. I will endeavor to state what I consider a reasonable explanation of the matter. Of necessity, I can merely state the general principles, my space preventing me from going into detail. I am compelled to use terms familiar to those who are acquainted with the theory of the dual minds, but it will be noticed that I use these terms as indicating varying forms of functioning of the same mind, and not as indicating that Man has two minds. I prefer the terms, Conscious thought and Sub-conscious thought to the other terms used by various writers on the subject, as I consider these terms clearer and as more nearly representing the truth. To the reader who has been accustomed to thinking of the Sub-conscious mind as the higher mind —the Soul, in fact—this chapter will prove somewhat confusing and perhaps disappointing. I must ask such a reader to withhold his judgment until he has carefully studied this and the next chapter. He will be able to do this more readily when he remembers that the Sub-conscious mind which some writers have exalted over its Conscious brother, is also spoken of by the same writers as being the mind that receives all sort of absurd suggestions in the hypnotic state, from the Conscious mind of another, and acts upon them. These same writers speak of the Sub-conscious mind as the Soul of Man, and then in the next chapter inform us that a man in whom the Sub-conscious is developed at the expense of the Conscious becomes a lunatic. If this be true, when a man's Soul leaves behind its Conscious brother, and passes into the state of pure Sub-consciousness, it becomes a lunatic, and the future life a Bedlam. These people are mistaking half-truths for Truth.

Beyond that which we speak of as Conscious and Sub-conscious, is something higher than either, which may be called the Super-conscious. I will take up that subject after I have discussed the Conscious and Sub-conscious functions of the mind. Do not confuse the attributes of the Super-conscious faculties with the manifestation of the Sub-conscious functions of the mind.

Man has but one mind, but he has many mental faculties, each faculty being capable of functioning along two different lines of mental effort. There are no distinct dividing lines separating the two several functions of a faculty, but they shade into each other as do the colors of the spectrum.

A Conscious thought of any faculty of the mind is the result of a direct impulse imparted at the time of the effort. A Sub-conscious thought of any faculty of the mind is the result of either a preceding Conscious thought of the same kind; a Conscious thought of another, along the lines of suggestion; thought vibrations from the mind of another; thought impulses from an ancestor, transmitted by the laws of heredity (including impulses transmitted from generation to generation, from the time of the original vibratory impulse imparted by the Primal Cause, which impulses gradually unfold, and unsheath, when the proper state of evolutionary development is reached).

The Conscious thought is new-born—fresh from the mint, whilst the Sub-conscious thought is of less recent creation, and, in fact, is often the result of vibratory impulses imparted in ages long past. The Conscious thought makes its own way, brushing aside the impeding vines, and kicking from its path the obstructing stones. The Sub-conscious thought usually travels along the beaten path.

A thought-impulse originally caused by a Conscious thought of a faculty, may become by continued repetition, or habit, strictly automatic, the impulse given it by the repeated Conscious thought developing a strong momentum which carries it on, along Sub-conscious lines, until stopped by another Conscious thought, or its direction changed by the same cause.

On the other hand, thought-impulses continued along Sub-conscious lines, may be terminated or corrected by a Conscious thought. The Conscious thought creates, changes or destroys. The Sub-conscious thought carries on the work given it by the Conscious thought, and obeys orders and suggestions.

The Conscious thought produces the thought-habit or motion-habit, and imparts to it the vibrations which carry it on along the Sub-conscious lines thereafter. The Conscious thought also has the power to send forth vibrations which neutralize the momentum of the thought-habit; it also is able to launch a *new* thought-habit or motion-habit with stronger vibrations which overcomes and absorbs the first thought or motion and substitutes the new one.

All thought-impulses, once started on their errands, continue to vibrate along Sub-conscious lines until corrected or terminated by subsequent impulses imparted by the Conscious thought or other controlling power. The continuance of the original impulse adds momentum and force to it, and renders its correction or termination more difficult. This explains that which is called "the force of habit." I think that this will be readily understood by those who have struggled to overcome a habit which had been easily acquired. The Law applies to good habits as well as bad. The moral is obvious.

Several of the faculties of the mind often combine to produce a single manifestation. A task to be performed may call for the combined exercise of several faculties, some of which may manifest by Conscious thought and others by Sub-conscious thought.

The meeting of new conditions—new problems—calls for the exercise of Conscious thought, whilst a familiar problem, or task, can be easily handled by the Sub-conscious thought, without the assistance of his more enterprising brother.

There is in nature an instinctive tendency of living organisms to perform certain actions; the tendency of an organized body to seek that which satisfies the wants of its organism. This tendency is sometimes called Appetency. It is really a Sub-conscious mental impulse, originating with the impetus imparted by the Primal Cause, and transmitted along the lines of evolutionary development, gaining strength and power as it progresses, grows and unfolds.

Man, the highest type of life yet produced upon this planet, shows the highest form of Sub-conscious mentation, and also a much higher development of Conscious mentation than is seen in the lower animals, and yet the degrees of that power vary widely among the different races of men. Even among men of our race, the different degrees of Conscious mentation are plainly noticeable, these degrees not depending, by any means, upon the amount of "culture," social position, or educational advantages possessed by the individual. Mental Culture and Mental Development are two very different things.

You have but to look around you to see the different stages of the development of Conscious mentation in man. The reasoning of many men is little more than Sub-conscious mentation, exhibiting but little of the qualities of volitional thought. They prefer to let other men think for them. Conscious mentation tires them, and they find the instinctive, automatic, Sub-conscious mental process much easier. Their minds work along the lines of least resistance. They are but little more than human sheep.

Among the lower animals and the lower types of men, Conscious mentation is largely confined to the grosser faculties—the more material plane, the higher mental factulties working along the instinctive, automatic lines of the Sub-conscious function.

As the lower forms of life progressed in the evolutionary scale, they unfolded new faculties, which were latent within them These faculties always manifested in the form of rudimentary Sub-conscious thought, and afterwards worked up, through higher Sub-conscious forms, until the Conscious thought was brought into play. The evolutionary process still continues, the invariable tendency being toward the goal of highly developed Conscious mentation.

This law of evolution is still in progress, and man is beginning to develop new powers of mind, which, of course, are first manifesting themselves along lines of Sub-conscious thought. Some men have developed these new faculties to a considerable degree, and it is possible that before long Man will be able to exercise them along the line of their Conscious functions. In fact, this power has already been attained by a few. This is the secret of the Oriental occultists, and of some of their Occidental brethren. We will have more to say on this subject in succeeding chapters.

The amenability of the mind to the Will may be increased by properly directed practice. That which we are in the habit of referring to as the "strengthening of the Will" is in reality the training of the mind to recognize and obey the Power Within. The Will is strong enough; it does not need strengthening, but the mind needs to be trained to receive and act upon the suggestions of the Will. The Will is the outward manifestation of the I AM. The Will current is flowing, in full strength, along the spiritual wires, but you must learn how to raise the trolley-pole to touch it before the mental car will move. This is a somewhat different idea from that which you have been in the habit of receiving from writers on the subject of Will Power, etc., but it is correct, as you will demonstrate to your own satisfaction if you will follow up the subject by experiments along the proper lines.

The attraction of THE ABSOLUTE is drawing man upward, and the vibratory force of the Primal Impulse has not yet exhausted itself. The time of evolutionary development has come, when man can help himself. The man who understands the Law, can accomplish wonders, by means of the development of the powers of the mind, whilst the man who turns his back upon the truth will suffer from his lack of knowledge of the Law.

He who understands the laws of his mental being, develops his latent powers and uses them intelligently. He does not despise his Sub-conscious mental expressions, but makes good use of them also, and charges them with the duties for which they are best fitted, and is able to obtain wonderful results from their work, having mastered them and trained them to do the bidding of the Higher Self. When they fail to do their work properly, he regulates them, and his knowledge prevents him from meddling with them unintelligently, and thereby doing himself harm. He develops the faculties and powers latent within him, and learns how to manifest them along the line of Conscious mentation as well as Sub-conscious. He knows that the *real* man within him is the master to whom both Conscious and Sub-conscious mentation are but tools. He has banished Fear, and enjoys Freedom. He has found *himself*. HE HAS LEARNED THE SECRET OF I AM.

CHAPTER VIII.

THE SUB-CONSCIOUS PLANE.

The greater part of our thinking performed along sub-conscious lines—
Illustrations of this fact—The sub-conscious, the habit plane—Means
by which the sub-conscious mentality is reached—A store-house of
thoughts—A mixture of wisdom and foolishness—How the super-
conscious faculties manifest first along sub-conscious lines—A reservoir receiving conscious thoughts—The desirability of a clear supplying stream—Auto-suggestions and affirmations—Did thought originate on the conscious, or sub-conscious plane?—My views on the
subject—Filling the store-house with proper material—Creating on
the thought plane—Our own thoughts, not others—Disease producing
on the sub-conscious plane—Thoughts take form in action—As a
man thinketh in his heart, so is he.

We are so accustomed to thinking of the mind as working
along conscious lines that it comes as a great surprise to us
when our attention is directed to the fact that the greater part
of the mental work being performed by us is being manifested
along sub-conscious lines. We are conscious of many of our
thoughts and many of our actions, but are almost or entirely
unconscious of thousands of thoughts and actions that are being
expressed every hour.

When we take nourishment in the shape of food we do it
consciously, but the process of digestion and assimilation is done
unconsciously, although the impulse causing it comes from the
mind just as much as if the act was consciously performed.
The food is converted into blood, and the blood is carried to all
parts of the body, and the various organs and parts of the body
are built up—all unconsciously. The heart beats—the stomach
digests—the liver and kidneys perform their functions—all unconsciously. But the work is done precisely—carefully—and
properly, under the direction of the mind working on the sub-
conscious plane. These things do not run themselves. The
mind controls them just as surely as if the work was done on
the conscious plane.

And so with many acts which we performed only with the
greatest care and trouble at first, but which afterwards we were
able to perform almost automatically. The woman who runs
her sewing machine—the painter who uses his brush—the work-
man who uses his tools—the operator who runs his machine—
all found their work required all their care and attention at first,

but now, the details of the work having been mastered, the work seems to be performed almost automatically—involuntarily—almost running by itself. Many a time have we been in a brown study and forgot the steps we were taking, and all at once when we awoke from our day-dream we found ourselves at the door of our home, the accustomed path having been followed unconsciously. I have seen men in a so-called "absent-minded state" cross crowded streets, passing before teams and carriages with the utmost carefulness and intelligence, who were totally unconscious of what they were doing, and who would look startled when told of the risks they had run. I have been told by skilled workmen that no man thoroughly understands his work until he can do it almost automatically. A man performing the same task every day acquires the "knack" of doing it, with scarcely a trace of conscious effort, or conscious attention. And yet no one would think of asserting that his fingers or hands, of themselves, possessed sufficient intelligence to do the work undirected by the brain. The unconscious impulse comes from the brain working on the sub-conscious plane of effort, and the work is directed just as intelligently as if the entire consciousness was focused upon it. This of course can only be done after the mind has acquired the habit of performing that particular task. Let something go wrong with the machine, and immediately the mind slips back to the conscious plane and undertakes the correction of the trouble.

The subconscious plane of the mind is practically the habit plane. As I have stated in the previous chapter, the subconscious plane of the mind can manifest only (1) something which it has previously learned from the conscious plane; (2) something which has been imparted to it by suggestion from another mind; (3) something which has been communicated to it from another mind, by means of thought-waves, etc.; (4) something which has been communicated along the lines of heredity, including impulses transmitted from generation to generation, from the time of the original vibratory impulse imparted by the Primal Cause, which impulses gradually unfold and unsheath, when the proper state of evolutionary development is reached.

The commonest habit of thought or motion may be along subconscious lines, and the same is true of some of the manifestations of the newly awakened superconscious faculties (of which we will speak later). The subconscious plane is a curious mixture of high and low; wisdom and foolishness; superstition and the highest philosophy. It is a storehouse of all sorts of mental furniture, tools, playthings, and what-not. On this plane may be found a curious conglomeration of wisdom and folly passed on from our consciousness, inherited from our ancestors, and acquired from those with whom we come in contact. This collection is being continually added to.

And this is not all. Every once in a while some superconscious faculty is awakened, perhaps only temporarily, and not having grown sufficiently to be taken up by the consciousness, it must manifest along sub-conscious lines. This has caused some writers to speak of the sub-conscious plane of the mind as the Soul, the "higher mind," etc., etc. Seeing genius and inspiration manifested along sub-conscious lines, they have imagined that there was a separate mind possessing all the higher faculties of the mind, and which they called the "subjective mind," the "sub-conscious mind," etc., etc. They were so carried away with the higher manifestations that they entirely overlooked the foolish, petty, nonsensical things to be found there—entirely forgot that their so-called "higher mind" was constantly amenable to suggestion and auto-suggestion from the conscious mind of the owner or of some other person. They did not seem to consider that the lower faculties of the mind manifested upon the sub-conscious plane, as well as the highest.

The sub-conscious plane of the mind, therefore, is very much what it has been made by past conscious thinking. A well-known writer, Henry Wood, of Boston, has compared it to "a reservoir or cistern into which there is flowing a small stream of conscious thinking." This being the case, it will be seen that the utmost care should be preserved in keeping the stream pure and clean. If one's mind has been polluted by allowing a stream of negative thought to pour into it in the past, the remedy is to be found in so changing the quality of the inpouring stream that it may be as clear as crystal, and the body of water in the cistern may gradually become clearer and clearer, until it is as pure and clear as the stream itself. And the greater the quantity of clear thinking we pour in, the sooner will the cistern be relieved of its foulness.

This is where auto-suggestion plays such a prominent part in the re-building of character, and in the development of the man. The auto-suggestions form a steady, strong stream pouring in and clearing the muddy waters of the mind. Whether we call them auto-suggestions, or affirmations, or statements, or declarations, it matters not. They are all the same thing, under different names.

There has been a dispute between students of the subject as to whether Man's knowledge came to him first through the sub-conscious plane and then reached the conscious, or whether he acquired knowledge through the conscious plane and then passed it on to the sub-conscious. Many good arguments have been advanced by both sides. Personally, it seems to me that both

sides are right. Many things that a man knows came to him
by the use of his conscious functions of the mind, and were afterwards passed on to the sub-conscious or habit plane. Other things
came to him, owing to the unfoldment of super-conscious faculties, first manifesting along sub-conscious lines, and then passing
into the field of consciousness. Then, after having been well
mastered, the knowledge was passed back to the habit-plane,
or sub-consciousness. Man often "feels" that a thing is so, before he "sees" that it is true; then after he "sees" it, and accepts
it intellectually, he passes it back again to the "feeling" plane,
stamped with the seal of approval of the "seeing" plane of mentation. I think that this will be plainer to you after you have
read the chapter on the Super-conscious faculties.

As Man advances on the Conscious plane, his store of Sub-
conscious knowledge becomes to a great extent the result of his
own Conscious mentation, and less the result of the thoughts
and suggestions of others. A man of limited reasoning ability—
one who uses his Conscious powers of thinking but little—has a
Sub-conscious store almost entirely composed of impressions
which he has obtained from others. The suggestions and thought-
impulses of others go to make up nearly his entire stock of knowledge. He has thought but little himself—in fact, scarcely knows
how to think for himself, and depends almost entirely upon
others for his mental concepts. As Man advances in reasoning
powers he thinks out things for himself, and passes along the
result of that thinking to the great sub-conscious store-house.
And such a Man realizes what he is—feels and recognizes the
existence of the Real Self, and begins to *create* on the thought-
plane. He is no longer a mere automaton—he has begun to
act for himself. And as he progresses this power grows. He
makes use of the Sub-conscious plane of thought, but he fills
the store-house with new, fresh, impressions and conclusions, and
gradually but surely eradicates the old negative, erroneous impressions that formerly filled his Sub-consciousness. A strong, vigorous, positive thought, sent fresh from the Conscious plane, will
neutralize a dozen negative thoughts that have been lodged in his
Sub-consciousness and which have been doing much to drag the
man down, and keep him down.

If we do not think thoughts for ourselves, somebody else's
thoughts and suggestions will fill up our sub-conscious store-
house, and we will be a creature of their thoughts, instead of
having a stock of self-made original thoughts. Many of us have
placidly accepted the world's thoughts of Fear, Superstition, Worry, Disease, Poverty, Narrowness, Condemnation, Bigotry, etc.,
without hesitation, and our mental store-house has been filled with
such trash. When we break our fetters and shake off our bonds,

and are free, then we dare to think for ourselves and we soon begin to stock up our Sub-consciousness with bright, fresh, new thoughts of our own, and the old negative thoughts find themselves crowded out or neutralized by the positive thoughts which are now pouring in.

New fields of consciousness are opening out before Man, and he is progressing rapidly in knowledge. He is drawing on the Super-conscious faculties for knowledge, and after bringing the results into the field of consciousness, he passes them along, mentally digested, to the Sub-conscious plane, to be used without effort whenever needed. All that which is in our Sub-consciousness is having a continual influence upon our lives, our actions, our health, our character. To a man whose Sub-consciousness has been filled with thoughts of disease it is the easiest thing in the world to become sick. Of course, all the work of producing the disease is on the Sub-conscious plane, and the work is done silently and quietly, but surely, all without his conscious knowledge. All at once he finds himself sick, without knowing how it happened. When he changes his front, and begins to steadily send healthy thoughts along to the Sub-consciousness, he finds that he no longer is troubled with the old complaints which formerly made life a burden to him. The Sub-consciousness no longer has the old materials to work with, and consequently starts to work and uses the new materials, and, instead of producing sickness, it builds up a strong, healthy body. ,

If you will carry in your minds the idea of the Sub-consciousness being a great store-house, filled with thoughts which you have passed along to it from the Conscious plane, and which thoughts are constantly manifesting themselves in action, you will be careful to allow nothing but the very best thought material to pass along to be stored up. You will refuse admittance to the negative thoughts arising in your own mind, and you will refuse admittance to the adverse suggestions of others.

What would you think of a man who was laying in a stock of supplies for the winter who would fill his cellars with poisonous foods, disease producing things, death-giving articles? You would think that he was worse than insane, would you not? And yet that is just what many of you have been doing. You have been filling up this storehouse of the mind with the vilest things. Poisons, deadly things, filthy objects, all of which have sooner or later injured you. Away with them. Cast them out. Fill their places with the strong, healthy thoughts which are coming into your minds since you have become acquainted with The New Thought. ,

Remember THOUGHTS TAKE FORM IN ACTION. This being true, what kind of thoughts do you wish to take form in action within you, and through you? Ask yourselves this question, and act accordingly. When you find yourselves thinking along a certain line, ask yourselves the question, "Do I wish this thought to take form in action?" If the answer is "Yes!" pass the thought along. If the answer is "No!" stop thinking along those lines at once and start to work thinking of things exactly opposed to the objectionable line of thoughts. Remember, a positive thought will always neutralize a negative thought. By a positive thought I mean a thought of Courage, Hope, Fearlessness, Determination—an "I Can and I Will" thought. By a negative thought I mean a thought of Fear, Worry, Hate, Malice, Disease, "I Can't," "I'm Afraid."

"As a man thinketh in his heart, so is he," is true for the reason that a man is largely the result of his store of Sub-conscious thoughts, and that Sub-conscious store is dependent to a very great degree upon what the Conscious thought has made it.

You are laying in your supplies of Thoughts, and these thoughts will sooner or later take form in action. Be careful in your choice. The best is none too good for you, and is just as cheap as the inferior grade. Use a little common sense and select a good supply of the best in the market.

CHAPTER IX.

THE SUPER-CONSCIOUS FACULTIES.

Faculties outside the realm of consciousness—Latent but unfolding—Super-
conscious faculties not a part of a sub-conscious mind, although
often manifested along sub-conscious lines—The distinction between
sub-conscious thoughts and those of the super-conscious faculties—
Above consciousness, not below it—Developing super-conscious faculties—The sub-conscious contains only what has been placed there—
The super-consciousness contains knowledge heretofore unrevealed
to Man—Drawing on the super-consciousness—What the super-
consciousness reveals to Man—What it has revealed—The most important truths come in this way—The higher psychic powers latent
within the super-consciousness—Productions which have "soul" in
them come from the super-conscious faculties—The dwelling place
of the Spirit—The Spirit and its domain—Recognition of the Spirit.

There are in the mind of Man many faculties which are outside of the realm of consciousness. They seem to be faculties
which have lain latent, and which, from time to time, are unfolded into the realm of consciousness. Of some of these faculties we have at the present time no actual knowledge; of others,
a few advanced men in all ages have become aware, and of this
class many of us are now catching occasional glimpses, but as
yet do not see clearly, and will not until the process of unfoldment
has progressed further. Other super-conscious faculties, which
were once hidden from man, have unfolded and we are becoming more and more aware of their existence.

Many writers have treated these faculties as forming a part
of that which they called the "Subjective Mind" or the "Sub-
conscious Mind," etc., but a little reflection will show that the sub-
conscious mentality only contains that which has been placed
there by the Conscious plane of the mind; the suggestions of
others, either verbal or by thought-transference, heredity, etc., or
by the reflection from these super-conscious faculties before they
have unfolded into the conscious plane. The sub-conscious mentality contains only that which has been placed there, while the
super-conscious faculties contain that which Man has never known
before, either consciously or sub-consciously.

Just as the sub-conscious field of mentation is below consciousness, so are these super-conscious faculties *above* consciousness.
And just as that which is on the conscious plane to-day will be
passed on to the sub-conscious to-morrow, so will much of that
which is now locked up in the latent super-conscious faculties

be unfolded into consciousness at a later period. Much that is now a part of our every day life was at an earlier stage in man's evolution a part of his super-consciousness and afterwards un-folded into its present consciousness, then was mentally digested and assimilated and passed on to the sub-conscious plane.

A man by concentration, meditation, and other means of spir-itual development may at times so awaken some of the latent super-conscious faculties that he will receive distinct impres-sions and knowledge from them, and will be able to use them. Many so-called mystics and occultists both in the Orient and the Occident have been able to accomplish this, but the majority of us have to be content with the occasional gleams, or the faint reflections, of the light coming from the unfolding faculties. Some of these faculties will not unfold until Man has reached a much higher plane of spiritual development than is now possi-ble; others are just beginning to unfold, and none but the most advanced has any knowledge of them, while others are now well under way in the unfoldment, and a greater number of peo-ple are becoming aware of this inner awakening every year.

A man who descends into the depths of his sub-consciousness finds only that which has been stored up there. This alone is enough to give a man a wonderful knowledge of the past—of the process of evolution—of much miscellaneous information which is stored up there—of things long forgotten by the con-scious mind—some say that even a memory of past lives may be obtained there by those who know how to look for it. But all that can be obtained from the sub-consciousness is what has been stored there. On the contrary, those who have been able to catch a gleam of that contained in the super-conscious faculties know that the knowledge so obtained is above man's experience. It is a glimpse into an unknown world—an illumination. The man who has caught a glimpse of the knowledge contained in some of the super-conscious faculties is a changed man—life is no longer the same to him—where before he believed, he now *knows*.

At the best, the little field of consciousness known to the average man, even if to it may be added the entire field of the sub-con-scious, it but small and petty. Most of the things which are the most important are outside of its scope, and his only knowledge of them comes to him as a reflection from the field of super-con-sciousness. Of course, the consciousness has grown—is grow-ing—by reason of the unfoldment of the super-conscious facul-ties, but Man has merely touched the outer edge of super-con-sciousness.

Man cannot tell, by the exercise of his conscious faculties, whether there is a GOD, the fact cannot be grasped by the con-scious mentality, and yet the faint glimpse of super-conscious-

ness makes him *feel* that there is a GOD, and as he progresses
he will *know* what he now feels. So it is with the question of
the immortality of the Soul. The consciousness cannot prove
it, and yet the super-consciousness makes us feel the truth of
what we cannot prove or see. And yet these two questions ex-
ceed in importance any other questions before us to-day. All
of our ethical principles—all of our morality—all of our plans
of life—are based upon these two facts, which we do not know
by reason of our consciousness, but which we *feel* are so because
of the gradual unfoldment of the super-consciousness. As this
unfoldment goes on our ideas of GOD become less crude—less
childish. We see him as a much greater Presence than ever
dreamt of by our forefathers, who could see in him but a magnified man, with all of man's failings, weaknesses and limitations. And Man of the future will have a concept as much
higher than ours as ours is higher than that of the savage.
And as this unfoldment goes on, our certainty of immortality
becomes stronger. It becomes more of a matter of knowing than
belief. In some of us the unfoldment has approached the field
of consciousness, and some have awakened into a state of consciousness of immortality.

Just stop to think for a moment, and consider from whence
come our feelings of Justice, Mercy, Love, Sympathy, Kindness. Not from the old consciousness surely. The Intellect does
not tell us these things. Why should man show Love or Com-
radeship or Sympathy for another, if the Intellect alone decides
the question? Why should not every man look out for himself and leave his brother to starve and suffer? Why should
he not trample his brother in the mire and take his belongings?
Is there anything in cold Intellect to tell you to do otherwise?
Not a thing—not a thing. Then why do you not do these things?
I'll tell you why. Because you *cannot*. Because from the inner
recesses of your Soul comes a protest. You do not stop to reason about the matter—you listen to the voice from within—gaze
at the light that comes from the unfolding super-consciousness.
But you say, all men have always had these feelings, and that
you do not see what unfolding super-consciousness has to do
with the question. Stop a moment! Did Man always feel thus?
Was human sympathy always as marked as to-day? Were men
always so broad in their love as to-day? No!—it is a gradual
unfoldment—a steady opening. We are to-day little more than
barbarians in some things, but we are growing as the unfoldment goes on, and some of these days it will be impossible for
us to do that which seems perfectly natural for us to-day. In
not so many years men will look back with amazement upon our
record of warfare, bloodshed, killing, exterminating, and all the

rest, and will wonder how a people of our intellectual development could have suffered these things to be done. They will view
our acts as we view the crimes of the arena of ancient Rome. And
our economic and social inhumanity to our brothers will seem hor-
rible to the men and women of that day. It will seem incredible to
them, as they will have reached a stage of spiritual unfoldment
which will render it simply impossible for them to do the things
which to-day seem perfectly natural and unavoidable to us. To
them the Brotherhood of Man will be no idle dream, but a live
everyday truth, worked out in their lives. They cannot avoid
this—it will come with unfoldment.

From this region of the super-conscious comes that which is
not contrary to reason, but which is *beyond* reason. This is the
source of the illumination—enlightenment—inspiration. This is
the region from which the poet obtains his inspiration—the writer
his gift—the seer his vision—the prophet his knowledge. Many
have received messages of this kind from the recesses of the super-
consciousness, and have thought that they heard the voices of
GOD—of angels—of spirits, but the voice came from within. In
this region are to be found the sources of intuition. Some of
these super-conscious faculties are higher than others, but each
has its own part to play.

Many of the higher psychic powers lie latent within the region
of the super-conscious. Some of us are able to use these gifts
to a greater or lesser degree, but to all but a few this use is always
more or less on the unconscious plane—we find it hard to manifest
psychic powers to order. But by practice, and by growth, these
gifts are brought within the realm of consciousness and we are
enabled to use them just as we would use any other faculty of the
mind or body. When man has attained this power he will have
mastered wonderful forces, and will have at his disposal instruments and tools of which but few dream at this time. It is a
wise provision of the Law that Man shall not acquire the use of
these powers until he is ready for them. When he is ready for
them, they come, and he then knows enough not to use them improperly. As the higher psychic faculties unfold, the spiritual
faculties also unfold, thus making it impossible for the possessor
to use his new found forces improperly. The man who aspires
to high psychic powers must come with clean hands and clean
heart. In truth, the very fact that he *seeks* power for the sake of
power, shows that he is not the proper possessor of these gifts.
It is only when he cares naught for power, that power comes.
Strange paradox—wonderful wisdom.

This field of super-consciousness is a source of the highest
happiness to the man who recognizes its existence, and who will
open himself to the knowledge coming from it, even though the

faculty be not fully unfolded. (You understand that the complete unfoldment of such a faculty brings it full into the field of consciousness, and it is no longer a super-conscious faculty, but belongs to our conscious mentality.) Many a man has received inspiration from within and has been given a message which astonished the world. Many poets, painters, writers, sculptors have acted upon the inspiration received from their super-consciousness. And you will notice that certain poems, certain writings, certain pictures, certain statues, have about them an undefinable something which appeals to us, and makes us feel their strength, which is absent from the productions of mere mental effort. Some of us are in the habit of saying that such productions have "soul" in them, and we are far nearer the truth than we realize when we say this. Some writers satisfy the intellect but fail to cause the reader to *feel*, while another writer will write a few verses or a short story and lo! the world is thrilled with the message. This is also true of the orator or speaker, who thrills an audience with a few simple words coming straight from the inner self, while a far more polished speaker attracts merely an intellectual interest.

Our super-conscious faculties are our only means of communication with the Centre of Life—with Higher Powers. Through them come the messages to the Soul. There are times when, through these faculties, our vision penetrates beyond the boundaries of personality, and our souls blend with and commune with the Divine. Through the channels of the super-conscious are we made acquainted with the Real Self—through them are we made aware of the I AM. Through the same sources are we made cognizant of the Oneness of things—of our relation to the Whole. Through them are we made sure of the existence and presence of GOD—of the immortality of the Soul. The only answers to the vital questions of Life and Existence are received through these channels.

In the inmost recesses of the super-consciousness is found the resting-place of the Soul—the holy of holies. Here dwells the Divine Spark which is our most precious inheritance from GOD —that which we mean when we say "the Spirit". It is the soul of the Soul—the centre of the Real Self. Words cannot convey an idea of the real meaning of the Spirit—to understand it one would need to understand GOD, for it is a drop from the Spirit Ocean—a grain of sand from the shores of the Infinite—a particle of the Sacred Flame. It is that part of us, toward the full recognition and consciousness of which, all this process of evolution, growth, development and unfoldment is tending. When we learn to recognize the existence and reality of the Spirit, it will respond by sending us flashes of enlightenment—illumination. As one grows in spiritual development he becomes accustomed to this

voice from within, and learns to distinguish it from messages from
the different planes of the mind—learns to follow its leadings,
and allows it to work through him for good.

Some men have so far developed in spiritual understanding that
they live the life of the Spirit—are led by the Spirit. The Spirit
is influencing all of us much more than we are aware, and we
can bring ourselves into a conscious realization of its leadings if
we will but trust it, and look toward it for light. I cannot attempt to go further into this subject, as it is something for which
one fails to find words wherewith to describe it. Those who have
awakened to an awareness of it, will understand what I mean,
and those who have not yet been made conscious of it would simply misunderstand me if I were to attempt to state an inward
feeling, foreign to their experience.

The Spirit is that within man which closest approaches the
Centre—is nearest to GOD. And when one becomes in close
conscious touch with it he feels his nearness to the Universal
Presence—he feels the touch of the Unseen Hand.

Many of you who read these words have had moments in your
lives, when you were for the moment conscious of being in the
awful presence of the Unknown. These moments may have come
whilst you were engaged in religious thought—while reading a
poem bearing a message from one soul to another—when on the
ocean and impressed with a sense of the greatness of the Universe—in some hour of affliction when human words seemed but
mockery—in a moment when all seemed lost and you were forced
to seek comfort from a power higher than yourself. But no matter how or when these experiences have come to you, there was
no mistaking their reality—no doubting the abiding sense of
peace, strength, and love of which you became conscious. In
these moments you were conscious of the Spirit within you, and
of its close relationship with the Center. Through the medium
of the Spirit, GOD makes himself known to Man.

CHAPTER X.

THE SOUL'S QUESTION.

Whence come I? Whither go I? What am I? What is the object of my existence?—Questions asked in all ages, in this and other worlds—The question absolutely unanswered for most men—Struggles for freedom—Climbing the mountain of Knowledge—The task begun, not ended—The spiritual hunger—Bread, not stones—The want is the prophecy of the means of satisfying it—The intellect will not answer the Riddle of the Universe—The answer must come from within—The Something Within—The development of Spiritual Consciousness—The intelligent Faith which knows, not merely understands—Unexplored regions of the Soul—Not contrary to intellect, but beyond it—A new world of knowledge opened out before the mental gaze—Joy insuperable.

"What am I? Whence come I? Whither go I? What is the object of my existence?" These questions have been asked by Man in all ages—all countries—all climes. And if the countless worlds surrounding the millions of suns in the Universe are inhabited—and I believe that they are—these questions have been asked there—have perhaps been answered by some of the dwellers of worlds wherein Life is manifested in higher forms than we have yet attained in this. All men have asked themselves this question—that is, all men who have attained to the stage where their minds recognized that a problem existed, for many men seem unaware of the existence of an unanswered problem—their mental vision is not clear enough for them to recognize that there is anything which needs an answer. To most of us the question remains absolutely unanswered—the smallest detail of the inquiry remains unsolved. We have cried aloud in agony of mind—have shouted to the Infinite a demand that we be told something of ourselves, but nothing comes back to us but the despairing echo of our own cry. As the poet has so pathetically expressed it:

> "For what am I?
> An infant crying in the night;
> An infant crying for the light;
> And with no language but a cry."

We are like the squirrel in the cage, who exhausts himself in travelling the long road of the wheel, only to find himself, at the end of his journey, just where he started. Or worse still, like the newly-caged wild bird, we dash ourselves against the bars of our mental prison, again and again, in our efforts to gain freedom, until at last we lie weak and bleeding, a captive still.

We have sought to climb the mountain of Knowledge, urged on by the thought of the place of blissful rest at the summit. We have toiled wearily up the steep and stony sides, and finally with bleeding hands and tired feet—with body and mind exhausted by our efforts, we reach the summit, and congratulate ourselves upon the ending of our task. But when we look around us, lo! our mountain is but a foothill—far above us, towering higher and higher, rise range after range of the real mountains, the highest peaks being hidden among the clouds.

We have felt that hunger for Spiritual knowledge that transcended the hunger for bread. We have sought this way and that way for the Bread of Life—and found it not. We have asked this authority, and that authority, for the bread that would nourish the Soul, but we were given nothing but the stone of Dogma and Creeds. At last, we sank exhausted, and felt that there was no bread to be had—that it was all a delusion, and a will-o'-the-wisp of the mind—that there was no reality to it. And we wept. But we forgot, that just as the hunger of the body implies that somewhere in the world is to be found that which will satisfy it—that just as the hunger of the mind implies that somewhere is to be found mental nourishment—so the mere fact that this Soul hunger *exists*, is a sure indication that somewhere there exists that which the Absolute has intended to satisfy it. The *want* is the proof of the possibility of the fulfillment. The trouble is that we have been seeking outside that which we can find only *within*. "The Kingdom of Heaven is within you."

If you prefer to try to solve the Problem of Life—the Riddle of the Universe—by scientific investigation, by exact reasoning, formal thought, mathematical demonstration—by all means follow this method. You will be taught the lesson of the power and the limitations of the human Intellect. You will travel round and round the circle of thought, and will find that you are but covering the ground over and over again. You will find that you have run into the intellectual *cul de sac*—the blind alley of Logic.

After you have beaten your wings against the cage of the Unknowable, and fall bruised and exhausted—after you have done all of which your Intellect is capable, and have thus learned your lesson—then listen to the Voice Within, see the tiny flame which burns steadily and cannot be extinguished, feel the pressure of the Somethin Within, and let it unfold. You will then begin to understand that as the mind of Man developed, by slow stages, from sensation to simple consciousness—from simple consciousness into self consciousness (in its lowest and highest degrees) so is there a consciousness in store for Man (and some few have attained it), higher than we have heretofore imagined, which is now beginning to manifest itself. You will then understand that there may be an Intelligent Faith which knows, not merely believes. These and other lessons you will learn in time.

As you progress along the lines of spiritual unfoldment you will find other sources of knowledge, seemingly apart from the Intellect, although, in reality, allied to it. You will find that there are regions of the Soul, heretofore unexplored, which you are invited to enter. You will find that you will be able to gain knowledge regarding these great questions which have defied your intellectual efforts, and although the information will not come to you through the door of the Intellect, yet it will not be repugnant to the Intellect. It will not be *contrary* to Intellect— but will be *beyond* Intellect. Instead of reaching the Ego through the portals of the Intellect, it will seem to come from a higher source—the Higher Reason—and will be then passed down to the Intellect, that the latter may assimilate it, and combine it with what it already has stored up. You will find that you have a new world of knowledge opened out before your mental gaze, and you will rejoice at the sight.

And, when you have reached the stage where you feel the promptings of the Higher Reason, and are able to live in accordance therewith, you will say with Edward Carpenter:

"Lo! the healing power descending from within, calming the enfevered mind, spreading peace among the grieving nerves. Lo! the eternal saviour, the sought after of all the world, dwelling hidden (to be disclosed) within each * * * * O joy insuperable."

CHAPTER XI.

THE ABSOLUTE.

God has begotten the Universe—The Universe has no boundaries or
limits—God manifested in every atom—The Causeless Cause—The
Intellect and its troubles—Man may spiritually know the reality of
God—Man's different concepts of God—God's attributes, Omnipo-
tence, Omniscience and Omnipresence, and their explanation—The
Father-Mother—The apparently conflicting ideas regarding God,
reconciled—God's manifestations: Substance, Energy, and Spirit—
All men really worshiping the one God, although apparently wor-
shiping many—A Personal God without the limitations of personality
—God manifesting in Infinite Spirit—In Infinite Energy—In Infinite
Substance—Man growing in God-consciousness—Nearer, my God, to
Thee—All are children of God, with a share of his attributes.

GOD has begotten and governs by Law that which we call the
Universe. And that Universe is not the petty thing that many
of us have been considering it to be. It is not the Earth as a
centre, with Sun, Moon and Stars circling around it, all designed
to contribute to the comfort, welfare and well-being of the inhabitants of that speck of dirt—the Earth. It is a Universe, the very
idea of which cannot be grasped by the human mind. It is Infinite. It has no boundaries, no limits. All parts of Space are
filled with manifestations of The Absolute. Countless Suns exist,
each having their planetary systems. Worlds are coming into
existence every day, and each day worlds are passing out of existence. Of course, when I say coming into existence, and going
out of existence, I mean that they are changing form—being gath-
ered together, or being dissolved. There is no destruction in
Nature—only change of form. Man in his egotism has imagined
himself to be the highest possible form of created life—has
thought of this tiny grain of matter, the Earth, as the only bit
of matter containing Life. When he realizes that there are millions upon millions of worlds containing Life in higher or lower
forms—when he realizes that this old Earth is but as a grain of
sand upon the sea-shore of the Universe—when he realizes that in
other spheres there exist beings as much higher than Man as
Man is higher than the amoeba—then he begins to realize the
comparative insignificance of Man and the greatness of GOD.

And then, when he begins to realize these things, he will begin
to acquire that spiritual consciousness that will make it evident
to him that he is on a long journey, and that wonderful possibili-

ties are ahead of him. He will realize that as he advances along the Path he will acquire new powers, new intelligence, new attributes, that will make him as a very god compared to his present state, although the grandest and highest state that he can imagine for himself will make him, as compared to GOD, only as a tiny speck of dust playing in the sunbeam as compared with the Sun itself.

GOD manifests himself in every atom of matter—in every atom of Energy—in every atom of Intelligence. His manifestations, although apparently innumerable, are all simply different manifestations of the same thing. There is really but One manifestation of GOD, taking upon itself countless forms and appearances. We are the expressions of GOD'S power, limited, it is true, but yet constantly growing, impelled upward by the attraction from above, and developing into a realization of our relation to all the other expressions of GOD, and to GOD himself.

GOD exists, has always existed, and will always exist. He is the only thing in the Universe that has no preceding cause. He is his own cause. He is the Cause of Causes. He is THE CAUSELESS CAUSE.

The human intellect, unaided, is incapable of grasping the idea of a thing without a cause, or of a cause without a preceding cause. The human intellect adheres closely to the doctrine of the universal law of cause and effect, and finds it impossible to discard it or to admit that there is a single exception to that law, as such exception would violate the law.

The intellect is forced to assume one of two things (1) that there is a *first* cause, or (2) that the chain of cause and effect is infinite. And either conclusion leaves the intellect in a poor position, because if it admits a *first* cause, its chain of cause and effect is broken; and if, on the contrary, it assumes that the chain of cause and effect is infinite, it is met with the fact that a thing that has no *beginning* can have no *cause*—that a *beginningless* thing is a *causeless* thing, besides which, as the Infinite cannot be grasped by the finite mind, it has, in its endeavor to avoid admitting that it could not explain things, given an explanation which it, itself, cannot grasp or understand. Poor intellect! It is the most valuable mental working instrument possessed by Man, yet when it makes the mistake of supposing that it *is* Man instead of one of his tools, it puts itself in a ridiculous position. It does not realize the wonderful possibilities before it, when, blended with the thought emanating from the higher planes of the Soul, it will produce results now scarcely dreamt of except by those who have reached the higher planes of consciousness.

Because the intellect has its limitations, we should not lose confidence in it, nor accept things told us by others which are con-

trary to intellect, merely because someone else claims these things
as truth. Accept the decision of the intellect, unless you receive
the truth from the higher consciousness, in which case it will not
be *contrary* to Intellect, but will merely go *beyond* intellect, teaching that which intellect cannot grasp by itself, and then calling on
intellect to do its part of the work in carrying out the mutual task.
Blind belief is a very different thing from inspiration—do not
confound them.

I feel safe in saying that the intellect, unaided, is incapable of
grasping the idea of a Causeless Cause, but our higher consciousness is aware of the existence of that which the intellect cannot
grasp. Because the intellect cannot conceive of a Cause without
a preceding cause, it does not follow that no such thing exists.
The blind man cannot image or understand color, but color exists.
The fish at the bottom of the sea cannot understand or image
things on land, but those things exist. Nor could a man form a
mental concept of Sugar, if he had never seen it or tasted anything sweet. It is all a matter of experience or consciousness, and
without these things nothing can be understood. The intellect,
recognizing all its limitations, is capable of deciding matters
within its own domain. When the time comes for us to know
things outside of the domain of the intellect, we find that we have
higher states of consciousness than we have heretofore deemed
possible, and we are able to make use of them.

On the intellectual plane of consciousness, everything of which
we have any knowledge has a preceding cause—every object a
maker. And consequently, the intellect, unaided, is unable to form
a mental concept of a thing without a cause—a thing without a
maker. This because it has had no experience of such a thing,
and has no consciousness of the existence of such a thing. Therefore, Man can never form an intellectual concept of GOD. He
may believe in GOD, because he feels conscious of his existence,
but he cannot through intellect explain or understand the mystery.
He will admit that GOD made Man, but he cannot answer the
child's question: "But who made God?" And yet he is unable
to form a mental concept of a thing without a cause—without a
maker. For his assurance of GOD'S existence he must go to a
higher source of consciousness. Many men believe in GOD because they have been told that he existed—others feel a dim perception of his existence—a *few* have attained to a *consciousness* of
his existence; they *know* it.

As Man grows in Spiritual Consciousness he grows to recognize more and more clearly the *reality* of GOD. From blind belief to a glimmering of consciousness, then to a clearer conception, then to a dawning realization, then to a *knowing* of his being; then to a faint understanding of his Law, and on and on

and on. GOD is not known through the intellect, but through the Higher Consciousness. And after He is known in this way, the intellect begins to reconcile the objects on its plane to the new conception. Until Man knows everything, he will have need of intellect to use as a tool, in connection with, and in harmony with, his higher source of knowledge. To a man who *feels* that GOD exists, no amount of argument to the contrary is of avail; and to the man who does not so *feel*, no amount of argument will create the feeling. It is something he must get from within, not from without. I am, of course, not speaking of any special conception of GOD. Some men who call it "Nature" have a higher conception of GOD than have others who think of God as a being with all the limitations of a man. Names matter nothing; it is the conception that shows what degree of God-consciousness a man has.

Mankind has had all sorts of ideas about GOD, ranging from that of the stick, stone or tree, to the graven image, sun, anthropomorphic being, up to higher concepts. But all men who ever worshiped a God, be it a stone, an idol, the sun, Joss, Baal, Brahma, Buddha, Isis, Jupiter, or Jehovah, worshiped in reality that Causeless Cause glimpses of which came to them distorted by the imperfections of mental or spiritual vision of the worshiper. The gods of the primitive man seem very small to us as we look back upon them, and the gods of their successors seem but a slight improvement, in fact, some of the latter were possessed of less desirable attributes than the cruder ideal. It has been said that a man's God is simply a magnified image of himself, possessing all the attributes of the viewer. This is but another way of saying that a man's concept of GOD is but a reflection of his own state of spiritual consciousness and mental development. As an object grows larger as one approaches it, so does GOD seem to grow as we draw nearer to him. And yet, in both cases the change is not in the object, but in ourselves. If you know a man's idea of GOD, you know what he is himself, or rather what state of growth he has reached.

The highest idea of GOD possessed by man carries with it the attributes of OMNIPOTENCE, OMNISCIENCE, OMNIPRESENCE. Many persons admit this, and use these terms lightly, without having the faintest conception of their real meaning. Let us see what these words mean, and then perhaps we will understand better what we mean when we say: "GOD."

OMNIPOTENT means all mighty; all powerful. This, of course, means that GOD is possessed of all power; that all power is his; not some power, but all power; that there is no other power, and consequently all power is GOD'S power. This leaves no room for any other power in the Universe, and consequently, all manifestations of power in the Universe must be forms of the power of GOD, whether we call the results of that manifestation of power "good" or "bad." It is all the power of GOD.

OMNISCIENT means all knowing; all wise; all seeing. It means that GOD is possessed of all knowledge; that he knows everything; that there is no place that he cannot see; no thing that he does not know; no thing that he does not understand fully. If there is the slightest thing that GOD does not know; if there is the slightest thing that he does not see; if there is the slightest thing he does not understand, then the word is meaningless. GOD knoweth, seeth and understandeth all things, and must have, for all eternity. Such a being cannot make mistakes; cannot change his mind; cannot act or deal unjustly. Infinite Wisdom is his.

OMNIPRESENT means all present; everywhere present at the same time. It means that GOD is present in all space; all places; all things; all persons; in every atom. If this is not true, then the word is meaningless. And if GOD is everywhere, there is no room for anything else. And if this is true, then everything must be a part of GOD—a part of a mighty Whole.

So you see that these words which we have been using so lightly, and carelessly, mean everything. When we can see and *feel* the meaning of these three words, then we are beginning to understand something about the greatness of GOD. We, of course, cannot grasp with our finite minds more than the most apparent parts of this great Truth, but we are growing, we are growing.

If we will accept these three words—attributes of GOD— Omnipotence, Omniscience, Omnipresence, as meaning just what they *do* mean, we open up our minds to a wonderful inflow of knowledge regarding the nature of what we call GOD. We are able to see harmony where inharmony reigned—unity where diversity was present—peace where conflict was manifested. We will receive a flood of light on the subject, illuminating places that were before shrouded in darkness—making clear and understandable many dark sayings.

With this understanding of these words, we will see that GOD is the sum of all knowledge, and that we cannot charge ignorance to him on even the slightest point, or the greatest problem. He KNOWS all that is to be known—all that can be known. We will also see that all power is his; that there cannot be room for any power outside of his power, for he has all the power there is or can be. We can conceive of no power opposing the all power. All power must be vested in GOD, and all manifestation of power must come from him. We will also see that GOD being everywhere, he must be present in all things, people, places—in US. We will see that GOD dwells in the humblest object—that we are all parts of the Whole—parts of GOD'S Universe. Small parts, it is true, but still parts—and even the smallest part is dear to the heart of the whole. The Whole is the sum of its parts, and all persons and things are but parts of the Whole. And no part can be greater than the Whole; and no part is equal to the Whole; and the Whole is the sum of the greatness of all its parts, Manifest and Unmanifest. And we, the Manifest, cannot understand the Unmanifest, to which the Manifest is but as the drop in the ocean.

All things are comprised in the idea of GOD—Spirit, Mind, Matter, Intelligence, Motion, Force, Life, Love, Justice. This idea of GOD—the Causeless Cause—has been held by men of all nations, tribes, races, countries, climes, ages. The sage, seer, philosopher, prophet, priest, scientist, of all times and peoples, here and there, scattered and few, saw this Truth—recognized the existence of the Whole, each expressing the thought by a different word. The religious man called this concept GOD; the philosopher and scientist, the First Cause, or the Unknowable, or the Absolute; the materialist, Nature; the skeptic, Life. And the followers of the different creeds have variously called it Jehovah, Buddha, Brahma, Allah, and many other names. But they all meant the same thing—GOD.

And this great Whole, of which we are parts, how shall we regard it? Not with fear, surely, for why should a part fear the Whole; why should the most humble atom in the body of the Universe fear the Soul that directed and governed the body? Why should the circumference fear the Center? When we realize just what we are, and what relation we bear to the whole, we will feel that "Love which casteth out all fear," for Him "in whom we live, and move and have our being."

In speaking of GOD, in this book, I have written the word in capital letters to indicate that I mean the broader, greater and grander conception of the Supreme, the Absolute, the Causeless Cause, in contra-distinction to the anthropomorphic idea of God—a being with all the limitations, finite intelligence, and childish ideas, passions and motives of a man. When I refer to the anthropomorphic idea of God—to a God bearing a personal name—I have written the word in the usual way. I have, you will notice, used the words "him," "his," etc., in referring to GOD, not because I consider him as being masculine or more like man than like woman, but merely because it is more convenient to follow the usual form and to avoid the use of the word "it," which we usually apply to inanimate or lower things. GOD has no sex. Or perhaps it would be better to say that he combines within himself both the Father-Mother elements, which appear separately in his manifestations. This idea of attributing to his God the attribute of the male alone, is probably explained by the fact that primitive man considered woman an inferior being, and preferred to think of his God as being like himself—a male. The mind of Man has instinctively revolted at this idea, and we find many races creating for themselves concepts of a female deity who reigns in connection with the male deity. The Catholic Church instinctively felt this, and the high place accorded the Virgin Mary was evidently the instinctive expression of this conception of the truth. I remember hearing of the story of a Catholic woman who was in great trouble and had sought the altar of the Holy Virgin for comfort. A Protestant, not understanding, asked her why she did not pray to God direct. She answered, "I feel better when praying to the Holy Virgin. She is a *woman* and can understand me better." When we remember how when in trouble, in childhood, we preferred to take our troubles to our mother rather than to our father, we can understand this feeling, and can better appreciate the motive inspiring the Catholic worshiper.

Of the inner nature of GOD, man can know practically nothing at this stage of development. He is just beginning to be conscious of his existence—just aware of his reality. He is just beginning to be able to grasp the meaning of the One Life—just able to see GOD by means of his manifestations. To some the idea of GOD appears that of some great impersonal Power—some great Infinite and Eternal Principle. To others GOD appears as a Personal God. To the first class the idea of imputing personality to GOD seems almost like sacrilege—a limitation of an illimitable principle—an idea belonging to the childhood of the race. To the second class, the thought of God as a Principle seems to rob Him of all feeling and love and compassion and understanding—seems like a conception of him as a blind Force or Principle like Electricity, Light, Heat, Gravitation, etc., and their souls revolt at the thought. They cry out that they are being robbed of their Loving Father, whose presence they have felt—of whose nearness they have been often aware.

Still another class—the Materialists—see The Absolute as Infinite and Eternal Matter, from which springs all things—of which all else is but an attribute or manifestation. This view while apparently satisfying to certain who hold to materialistic teachings, is most repugnant to those who feel that Matter is the crudest form of the manifestations of GOD.

Strange as it may appear to those who have not grasped the Truth, all of these views are partly correct and yet none of them is entirely correct. The Divine Paradox manifests itself here.

Those who have caught a glimpse of the Truth, know that

GOD himself is beyond the highest conception of the mind of Man to-day, but they also know that he manifests himself in three different ways: (1) SUBSTANCE, or matter; (2) ENERGY, or force; (3) SPIRIT, Intelligence, or Mind. All of these terms are unsatisfactory, but the terms: Substance, Energy, and Spirit, are the best available terms with which to attempt to explain an unexplainable thing.

GOD in his three manifestations gives us Infinite and Eternal Spirit; Infinite and Eternal Energy; Infinite and Eternal Substance. To those who prefer to think of GOD as a personal God, the manifestation of Infinite and Eternal Spirit appeals most strongly and satisfies the cravings of their soul. To those whose intellects have refused to be satisfied with the conception of GOD as a Person, and yet who are unwilling to think that there is nothing but manifestations of Matter, the manifestation of Infinite and Eternal Energy satisfies the intellectual demand. To those whose hearts no longer crave the belief in a Divine Father, and who can see nothing but Matter as the cause of all life, the manifestation of Infinite and Eternal Substance seems to explain all.

When we realize that no matter whether we be Materialists, Occultists, or orthodox believers, we are all, in reality, looking to the same Causeless Cause—GOD—as seen through some particular manifestation, we will cease to find fault and abuse each other. We will see that we are all children of the same Father—all brothers and sisters looking to that Father as the source of our being and as our strength and comfort. We will then get, for the first time, the real idea of the Fatherhood of God and the Brotherhood of Man.

The savage who bows down to a few sticks and feathers—the heathen who bows down to the graven image—the sun worshiper who worships the glorious center of the solar system—the primitive man who worships the God he cannot see, and which God is merely a reflection of himself—the man who has developed and worships a high ideal of a personal God—the followers of Judaism, Brahmanism, Buddhism, Mohammedism, Confucianism, Taoism, the differing sects of the Christian church in all their many and varied forms—all worship their conception of GOD—all feel the impelling attraction toward GOD—all instinctively know that he exists, although their minds see him through cloudy glasses or clearer glasses, according to their development—all are doing the best they know how. And the scientist who finds himself confronted with what he calls the First Cause, Nature, or the Unknowable—and the Materialist who sees Matter as All—all have their faces turned toward GOD.

GOD is all that one can conceive of a personal God, and more.

He is the personal God without the limitations of personality.
He comprises all that we have loved to look for in a personal
God, and more. He is the God we have always worshiped,
but now that we are nearer to him we see that he is much greater,
much grander, much more Divine than we had ever conceived
him as being. He is all that we could wish, and yet more. He
combines the love of Father, Mother, Brother, Sister—yea the
love of every human relation—and yet these attributes are but
as an atom of his capacity for Love. In the manifestation of
Spirit, GOD fills our every expectation, wish, hope and desire,
and then far transcends them. The finite cannot begin to grasp
the Love of the Infinite.

And GOD in his manifestation of Energy comprises all the
Energy and power that can be conceived of by man—and more.
All Energy and Power is that of GOD. He is Omnipotent—all
powerful.

And GOD in his manifestation of Spirit, is Omniscient. He
possesses all knowledge. There can be no knowledge outside of
himself. He is the sum of all Knowledge and Wisdom. He
makes no mistakes—he changes not his Mind—he repents not—
he learns not—he KNOWS and has always known.

And GOD in his manifestation of Substance, is Omnipresent—
his Substance is everywhere, and there is no other Substance.
The Materialist is correct when he states that Matter is Omnipresent—present everywhere—but he mistakes the manifestation
for that which lies back of it—the manifestation for the mani-
festor.

The metaphysician, the occultist and the physical scientist have
arrived at the same stage. From their differing points of view
they see that Spirit, Energy and Substance (or as the scientists
term them, Intelligence, Force and Matter) are Infinite and
Eternal. Many have agreed upon this point, and have been
unable to analyze further. They have stated that there were
these three Principles in the Universe, and that further back they
could not reason. They are right, but they fail to see that these
things are not Causes but are the manifestation of the One—the
Causeless Cause—GOD.

We cannot form the faintest idea of GOD except through his
three manifestations, and their combinations. We are just reaching the stage in mental development where we are beginning to
understand some little about these manifestations and their laws.
We are just beginning to avail ourselves of our little knowledge
regarding them, and are learning to turn our knowledge to ac-
count, in the direction of making use of some of the wonderful
forms of Energy which we have discovered. We have, as yet,
only the most elementary knowledge of these manifestations of

GOD, and we might go on for millions of ages, and still be in the kindergarten stage. And until we can at least faintly grasp the meaning and nature of these wonderful manifestations of GOD itself, we cannot hope to even dimly imagine that which lies behind them—GOD himself.

And why attempt to fathom the unfathomable at this time? Why attempt to master the higher mathematics of life, when we are just learning that two and two make four? What folly. Let us learn as much about these manifestations as we can—let us grow into the broader knowledge of them that is coming to us from without and from within—and rejoice. Let us look forward to the worlds we have still to conquer—the ages of blissful knowledge that lie ahead of us—and be glad. Let us rejoice and shout that at last we have found the Path—and let us travel it with confidence and courage and joy.

Let us not weep, now that we have found that GOD is so much greater than we ever dreamed of. Let us not feel that he has been set so much farther away from us, for such is far from being the case. When we once get our new bearings, we will see that as our idea of GOD has grown, we, ourselves, have grown in proportion. Let us realize that with the consciousness of the existence of GOD we have gained a consciousness of being nearer to him—of being a part of The Whole—of not being merely *created* by GOD, but of being *begotten* of him—as possessing an atom of his spirit—a portion of his Substance—a particle of his power—of being *of* him, and not from him—of being a part *of* Him, and not apart from him. And let us know that as we grow, unfold and develop, we will acquire a greater share of all of his attributes, Knowledge, Power, and command over Space. Let us remember that we are begotten of him, and as the child possesses all the qualities of the Father, in a less developed form, so do we, the Children of God, possess a particle of each of His attributes. Think of it for a moment, and then remember that we are GROWING.

"Thou great eternal Infinite, the great unbounded Whole.
Thy body is the Universe—thy spirit is the soul.
If thou dost fill immensity; if thou art all in all;
 If thou wert here before I was, I am not here at all.
How could I live outside of thee? Dost thou fill earth and air?
There surely is no place for me outside of everywhere.
If thou art God, and thou dost fill immensity of space,
Then I'm of God, think as you will, or else I have no place.
And if I have no place at all, or if I am not here,
'Banished' I surely cannot be, for then I be somewhere.
Then I must be a part of God, no matter if I'm small;
And if I'm not a part of him, there's no such God at all."
—*Anonymous.*

CHAPTER XII.

THE ONENESS OF ALL.

There is but One—God's manifestations apparently innumerable, but in reality but One—Universal Oneness—Centre and circumference— The rays from the Centre reach all parts of the circle—High and low; beautiful and hideous; exalted or depraved; all a part of the One—Separateness but an illusion—God the only standard of perfection—Individuality does not decrease but grows—Beginning to understand—Truth everywhere—Sin the result of a belief in separateness —Invariable laws in operation—The fundamental consciousness of religion—The Universal Presence—The Oneness of All explains psychic mysteries, and relationships between persons and things— Human sympathy growing—The point towards which the race is traveling.

"There is but One." GOD'S manifestations are apparently innumerable, but from the Cosmic view All is but One, in the last analysis. The mind cannot grasp this idea fully without the aid of symbols, or figures of speech. The man of the Cosmic knowing is conscious of this Oneness of All but cannot clearly express it in words to others. The mind creates a symbol in an attempt to express the inexpressible. The mystics have attempted to express this idea of Oneness by a symbol—a circle with a central point, with rays emanating from the central point and reaching to the circumference, touching it at all points.

The circle represents the Universal Oneness, the central point representing the Central Intelligence, Power, Presence—GOD— surrounded by his emanations. This symbol is inadequate, for the pictured circle has dimensions—there is something outside of it. The circle of GOD'S emanations has no such dimensions —no such limitations—and *there is no outside*. All is included and nothing is left out. There is no *out*—all is *in*. And, in the symbol, the rays emanating from the Center have spaces between them, leaving some part of the space uncovered by the rays, while in reality the Central rays touch and cover every part of the emanated Universe—there is no place, person, or thing not in touch with the Center—not in communication with GOD. GOD'S Love, Presence, Power, and Spirit reach all, and are still a part of him, just as the rays of the sun spread in all directions and are still parts of the sun. But any symbol, figure of speech, or form of expression is inadequate. The inexpressible cannot be expressed. The finite cannot express the infinite.

All is One. The most beautiful thing—the most loathsome object; the life-giving draught from the crystal spring—the most deadly poison; the beautiful mountain—the destroying volcano; the spiritual man—the bloated drunkard in the gutter; the man teaching and living the highest Truth—the murderer awaiting the gallows; the noblest type of womanhood—the leering denizen of the pavement; the harmless dove—the venomous cobra; all are included in the circle. None is left out—none *can* be left out. We must include the lowest as well as the highest. On other planes of life are radiant creatures as much higher than Man, as we know him, as Man is higher than the amoeba. And on still other planes are forms of life lower than any known to us. And they likewise are included. They are all in the circle—archangel and elemental form. They are one with us—the higher and the lower. And the higher know, and do not shrink from the relationship—nor does the man who sees the Truth shrink from the relationship. All is One. And the One is in All.

Separateness is but an illusion—a dream of the undeveloped consciousness. As man unfolds into the Cosmic Knowing, he sees the folly of the idea of Separateness—of exclusion—of condemnation—of any real difference between parts of the Whole. He sees degrees and grades—stages of growth—planes—but no real difference in the last analysis. He sees that GOD alone is perfect—that all the rest is but relative. As the Center is approached, the approaching thing rises in the scale. And the farther away from the Center the thing is, the lower in the relative scale does it appear. But higher or lower, it is a part of the Whole—a thing begotten by GOD. The only standard of perfection is GOD.

Each is a part of All. Not only a part, but a part intimately related to, and connected with, every other part. And All is in continual motion—constantly advancing—progressing—developing—unfolding—nearing the Center. All Life is on The Path. And as the part progresses along The Path, it becomes more and more conscious of its connection with All, and with the Center—realizes more and more the lack of separateness, and the Oneness of things. This consciousness is the proof of the stage of the journey which has been reached by the traveler—the milestone on The Path. The consciousness of Individuality does not decrease—on the contrary, the Individuality enlarges—grows—takes on more substance. The traveler sees his relationship to, and his connection with, a larger and larger part of the Whole, until, far along The Path, he becomes conscious of his nearness to All, and the sense of separateness passes away, never to return. The traveler along The Path may rest for long periods—may even wander from The Path, and be apparently lost—but he never turns backward—and stray away as he may, he always returns.

When one begins to see things as they are, he becomes aware of rapidly broadening sympathies and understanding. Prejudice after prejudice drops away, until the vision is clear. One then begins to "understand." He sees in others that which is in himself—he sees in himself that which is in others. And he loses the feeling of superiority—and he ceases to condemn. He pities, but does not condemn. He has a broader insight into the motives of men—a clearer insight into their weaknesses, their temptations. He sees them as fellow travelers on The Path—some a little ahead, some a little behind—some stumbling and soiling themselves with the dust and mire of the road—but all travelers on The Path, all journeying toward the same place.

He sees *some* Truth in all sciences, all religions, all philosophies, but knows that none of them has *all* the Truth. The Truth is too great and large a thing to be held in one place—or by any one person. All have a bit of it. When one realizes this, he sees the folly of the bickerings, jealousies, condemnation, prejudices, and bitterness between people of differing beliefs—adherents of different faiths. He recognizes that they are all looking toward the Truth from different points of view—that all are doing the best they know how—all are reporting the Truth as they see it. As the feeling of separateness drops away, so does the feeling of opposition and difference pass.

To one who has this sense of Oneness, the world broadens out immeasurably, in fact to such a one, the Universe is the world, and all that it contains seems akin to himself. All men are his brothers—all places his home—all pleasures are his—all pain, his pain (though, in reality, not pain at all)—all life, his life. He feels close to everything—man, beast, plant, mineral—all are parts of the One.

And such a one sees that all that we have been calling "sin" arises from the sense of separateness—a lack of recognition of the Oneness of All. When Man finally sees that All is One, and that separateness is but an illusion, he will find it impossible to "sin." The relation of man to man will then be adjusted on the basis of the Oneness of All, and injustice will then be impossible. The sense of separateness is responsible for Man's woes—distress—misery—selfishness—lack of Human Brotherhood. In the day that is coming, Man's law will have outlived its usefulness and will be forgotten. The Divine law of Oneness will be written in the hearts of men, and will form an unfailing guide. The welfare of one will be the welfare of all. The Fatherhood of GOD and the Brotherhood of Man will be living truths and principles of action. There will be but one code of ethics and morals, and that will be engraved on the heart of Man.

Throughout that part of the Universe with which we are acquainted, we perceive that invariable laws are in operation—everywhere the same. From the humblest form of life to the highest, all are under the Law. And from what we know of the Oneness of All, we know that these same laws are in operation throughout all the Universe, on and on and on—always the same. The suns, surrounded by their systems, obey the same law that controls the movements of the tiniest atom of matter.

All is One, and yet the variety of manifestation and expression is infinite. Each is a part of the Whole, and yet the Whole expresses itself differently in each. The separate experience of the part goes to make up the combined experience of the Whole.

Men differ in details, yet in the main agree upon the essentials. Take all the different forms of religion and analyze them, and what do you find after discarding the useless material? Simply this—a consciousness, coming from within, that there is, back of all things, and *in* all things, a Universal Presence which loves that which has emanated from it. This is the fundamental consciousness of religion. What more do you want? All the rest has been built around it by Man's ignorance, conceit and desire to rule his fellows by a show of superior knowledge. Around this Divine Spark, priest-craft has built temples intended to shelter it, but which really have almost shut it out from view. Tear down the obstructions and gaze fearlessly and without hindrance upon the Light of the Spirit.

And, as Man gazes at the Light, he grows conscious that all the Universe is pervaded by that Universal Presence—that the Universal Intelligence knows all—that the Universal Power is everywhere in operation—that All is One—All an emanation of GOD.

When this idea of Oneness of Life is recognized, one begins to understand the wonderful relationships between persons and things—the psychic mysteries of Telepathy, Thought-transference, Clairvoyance and other phenomena of that kind. All that which is included in what we call The New Thought is understandable only when this idea of Oneness is grasped. Many dark places are illumined—many hard sayings understood—many difficult facts assimilated and absorbed—when we recognize this idea of Oneness.

Human sympathy, love, affection, pity, compassion, tenderness, brotherly love, humanity, are understood in no other way. As man grows into this understanding his sympathies increase. At the beginning, Man cared only for himself; then for himself and family; then his tribe was included; then the confederation of

tribes; then his principality; then his nation; then friendly
nations; then nations with whom he was brought into contact;
and so on and on, until finally he will feel a brotherly feeling
for all mankind, and wars between different peoples will be
no more. As he grows in the idea of Oneness, unconsciously
at first, he grows in sympathy. As Man progresses in the scale,
his sympathies broaden, and his prejudices disappear.

This is the point toward which the race is traveling. Some
individuals have stepped a little forward, and are deemed vision-
aries by the mass of people. Others have dropped to the rear, and
lag along, the mass of people considering them barbarous and
devoid of human kindness. But all are moving forward. The
knell of Selfishness is being sounded—a better day is dawning
for Man as he marches onward. The day of Universal Peace
and Human Brotherhood may seem afar off, but we are approaching it. Amid the noise of Materialism, Cupidity, Selfishness and Greed, there is another note being sounded. It is not
loud, but it is clear and strong, and is constantly growing in
volume. Men are stopping to listen, and wondering what it all
means. Soon they will find that the clear note is vibrating
through them, and they will rally around the standard which is
heralded by that note. And the note will then be so piercing
and world-filling that the legions of Mammon and Selfishness
will drop their arms and be irresistibly drawn along with the
rest. This is not a dream—it is a prophecy of the future. Man
cannot escape this. It may come with pain and suffering—but
come it must. The note is sounding. Listen to it. It is swelling
and growing in strength. Soon it will fill the world. And when
a man hears it he will understand, and will await anxiously the
day when he will find it possible to lay down the weapons with
which he has been fighting his brother, not only on the battle-
field, but in the market-place. He will hail with gladness the
coming day, when he will be relieved from the struggle con-
sequent upon his constant attempt to rob his brother, and at the
same time keep another brother from robbing *him*. He will hail
the day when Love, not Fear, will rule. These things are coming
to pass because of the consciousness of the Oneness of All unfolding within the minds of men.

It is hard when we grow to see the folly of all this selfishness
and struggle of brother with brother, and yet find ourselves unable to escape from it. No one can escape until all escape, but
each one who grows to feel and understand, forms one of a
growing army, which will sooner or later form a majority.
Some day the race will be astonished to find how many of its
number are ready for the new dispensation, and then will rise

a joyous shout of deliverance and the mutual strife will have ended. Speed the day.

In that day the teachings and philosophy of Christ will be found to be practical and practicable, and the spirit of the Master's teachings will be lived up to. Men will no longer fear to live out these teachings which they now profess to believe but pronounce "impractical" as principles of living. Then will the Sermon on the Mount be capable of realization—then will the Golden Rule be in every man's heart and mind. With the consciousness of the Oneness of All comes the true conception of Christ's mission, and the belief in its ultimate fulfilment.

CHAPTER XIII.

THE IMMORTALITY OF THE SOUL.

Man IS, and will be—Life continues—The "I" is the Soul—Higher and lower forms of life—Life on different planes—Metempsychosis or Reincarnation—A higher view of the subject—The Soul has existed for ages—Progressing from lower to higher forms, and still progressing—Theories not fundamental when the consciousness of immortality is reached—Living in the Now—Universal Law—Man's concepts changing as he grows—We are babes in understanding, compared with those who have reached higher planes—Angels and archangels—The Universe filled with forms of life, in different stages of development—Man but a manifestation of the Soul in one particular stage of development—Paul, the mystic, and his view.

Man IS. He lives and always will live. He cannot die. The thing that we call Death is no more death than is the sleep into which we sink at night, and from which we emerge in the morning, refreshed, brightened, and strengthened. It is a temporary loss of consciousness—nothing more. And Life is continuous—continuous progression, unfoldment and development. There are no sudden breaks—no startling changes—no miraculous transformations. All is steady growth.

To many who believe that they will live beyond the grave, it seems as if something which they call "my soul" will arise from the ruins of their body and will live on forever. To those in whom spiritual consciousness has been awakened, a different concept presents itself. They feel the I AM consciousness strong within them, and know that, no matter what may happen to the body, the Real Self will live on. They know that that which they call "I" is the soul, and are not deceived by the thought that the soul is something that is going to put in an appearance after the "I" lies down in death. Stop and think for a moment. There is every difference between the two concepts. The whole question hinges on this distinction. The Soul is not a thing apart from yourself—it is YOU—YOU are the Soul.

> "Lord of a thousand worlds am I,
> And I reign since time began;
> And Night and Day in cyclic sway,
> Shall pass while their deeds I scan.
> Yet time shall cease, ere I find release,
> FOR I AM THE SOUL OF MAN."
> —*Orr.*

It is YOU who lives on forever, not some intangible thing that develops from you at the hour of death. This YOU is living in eternity as much now as it ever will be. This is Eternity —right NOW. Many of us, before we grow into an understanding of things, feel that this life is of no consequence—that it is a miserable thing and that true living will not begin until we get out of the body and become a Spirit. Why, you are a Spirit as much now as ever. It is true that you have a body of flesh, and that at some future time you will not be so burdened. But you may rest assured that you have a body because you *need* a body—because in this stage of growth a body is indispensable to your development. When you outlive the necessity of a body, you will be relieved of it. And then there are bodies and bodies. Those among men, who in all ages have kept alive the flame of esoteric knowledge, have taught that on other planes of existence—in other worlds—there were beings who had bodies far more ethereal than the ones we use. And also that on lower planes of life were to be found beings whose bodies were far more material and gross than the ones furnished us. They have taught that when we had lived out the experiences of Earth-life, and had fitted ourselves for life on a higher plane, we would pass on to the higher plane and would incarnate in bodies suited for our advanced stage of development. And they also taught that before we had incarnated on Earth, we had dwelt elsewhere, using bodies fitted for our development at that time, which bodies were far lower in the scale than those we now have. The body is always the instrument of the Soul, and the Soul is given the instrument best fitted for its stage of development.

Some schools teach the doctrine of Metempsychosis, or Reincarnation, as it is more generally termed. They believe that after death we return to occupy another earthly body, to which body we are attracted by the law of attraction or Karma. I have always felt that there was much in this idea, although I have also felt that some of its advocates have claimed too much for it. It is indisputable that in the theory of Metempsychosis there is found the only possible explanation of the inequalities and apparent injustices of life. It is the only theory that squares with Justice. But to assume that Life is merely one round of repeated earthly incarnations in bodies as we know them—here on Earth—is to take but a narrow view of the subject.

I believe that the Soul has existed for ages. I believe that it has always existed as a part of the Whole, and that manifested as a separate, or apparently separate entity, it has existed for untold ages, working its way upward through different forms of expression, from lower to higher, always progressing—always growing. And I believe that it will continue to progress and grow and unfold and develop during the ages, progressing

from lower to higher forms, and then on to higher and higher
and higher. The man who has unfolded sufficiently to get a
glimpse of that which is hidden in his Soul, is enabled to see a
little ahead of his fellows—is able to pierce the darkness for a
short distance—but beyond that he cannot see. A few have
been able to grasp truths apparently far beyond the understanding of the multitude, but even this is as nothing compared to
the Whole Truth. GOD'S plan is revealed to Man only as Man
is able to grasp it. As Man grows in spiritual understanding,
there will be found new portions of the Truth awaiting him.

It does not make much difference whether one believes in
Metempsychosis or whether he does not. At the best it is not
worth while disputing about. When the consciousness of Eternal Life comes to one he does not care how many bodies he may
have used as he progressed along the Path, or how many more
he may have occasion to use before he passes on to a higher
plane. He does not care much for these things, except as a
matter of speculation. He knows that he IS, and always will
be. He feels that every moment is NOW and he lives it out.
He knows that he cannot be destroyed, or annihilated. He knows
that the smallest thing in the Universe is governed by the Universal Law—that GOD is aware of his existence and is fully
cognizant of all that befalls him. He knows that he cannot be
blotted out—cannot be separated from the whole—cannot be
placed outside of the Universe—cannot be forgotten or ignored.
And knowing these things, he does not fret about what is before
him. He knows that whatever it is, it must be GOOD. He
knows that the Universe is very large, and that there is plenty
of room for him somewhere in it, and that the very best place for
him will be the particular place where he will be found at any
time. He knows that he cannot escape his own good—that he
cannot get away from GOD. And knowing these things, he
is content—he lives on, day by day, enjoying the play of life
in him and around him.

Whether future growth is to come through additional incarnations on this earth, or in other worlds, or whether the Soul
once released from the bonds of earthly flesh, goes into other
planes of existence, there to grow, is not fundamental—not material. The Universe is large, and it is just possible that we may
be given an opportunity of visiting all parts of it in our development, in which case it would seem that we are on a comparatively low plane of life just now—are just awakening into
a consciousness of what it all means, and in the future we will
be conscious of our growth and progress and development. A
babe grows and develops, without knowing anything about it.
Then it becomes self conscious and grows in understanding, and

remembers and thinks and draws conclusions. And so it may
be that we are in the infantile stage of spiritual development, and
are just beginning to "notice."

Fretting about the future life is as unprofitable a thing as
worrying about next week, or next month, or next year. The
man of attained growth regards one as ridiculous as the other.
Neither accomplishes any good. The true philosophy is to live
in the NOW. Don't you bother yourselves about the future life.
Better leave that in the hands of GOD. He takes everything
into consideration—foresees all obstacles—knows all about you
and your requirements—and really is able to conduct the affairs
of the Universe without any particular suggestions from you.
Man's ideas about the hereafter change from time to time as
he grows. Some of the old ideas were very childish, and some
of our best ideas no doubt appear just as childish to the minds
of beings who have attained the higher stages of existence.
What babes in understanding we must appear to some of those
radiant creatures who have long since passed along the Path
that we are now treading, and have reached the stage of spiritual
manhood. Where these beings are and what is their state, I do
not know, but I feel very confident that they exist, and that it
is a part of GOD'S plan to allow them to lend a helping hand
to those who are in our stage of development.

I believe that the old doctrine of angels and arch-angels was
founded on truth, and was but man's imperfect way of expressing
a fact in the spiritual world beyond his comprehension. We,
in our conceit, are apt to imagine that GOD exhausted his creative power in supplying the earth with the forms which we
see around us, and that there are no other forms of life anywhere
else in the Universe. This is an idea about as absurd as that
formerly possessed by man, namely, that this little earth—this
grain of sand—was the center of the Universe and that the sun
and moon and the stars were made for the sole benefit of a certain
one of its inhabitants called Man. Man has graduated out of
that idea, but still clings to the equally absurd notion that the
earth is the center of spiritual life, and that Man as we know
him is the highest and only creature having a soul. Men will
see later on that GOD'S Universe is large, and that this world
of ours is very small in comparison with the whole, and that Man
as we know him is but a manifestation of the Soul in one particular stage of development. These may seem like hard sayings
to some, but they will gradually grow into an understanding of
them. Man—the real Man—is a wonderful being, but Man in
his present form of expression, is an undeveloped, crude, gross
and primitive creature.

I have not attempted to present a theory of future life. I

have my own views on the subject, and have hinted at them here,
but I have no desire to force any special theory upon you. If
you have a theory or conception that gives you comfort and
satisfaction, by all means hold to it. The chances are that we
are *all* right, but that no one of us is *altogether* right in his conceptions. I do not see how Man, in his present stage of development, can attempt to conceive of the details of future
existence. He can see a little further into the darkness, but he
cannot grasp more than a bare idea of the truth. I think that
when one has awakened to the consciousness of eternal life—
when he feels sure that he LIVES—that he IS—he will not at-
tach much importance to theories regarding the details or ar-
rangements of the future life. He will feel perfectly safe in
trusting to the Law. I think that Paul, the mystic, summed
up the matter when he said: "We are all sons of God, but what
we shall be does not as yet appear."

CHAPTER XIV.

THE UNFOLDMENT.

Man's development along the lines of unfoldment—The power within—A mighty force—Developing and unfolding like a plant—Life is growth Within and Without—The Divine Paradox—Action and reaction—The internal urge and the external obstacles, both factors in development—Relative and Absolute—The final, or ultimate, effect or product, is the underlying cause of the unfoldment—Man the effect, is Man the Cause—In Man of to-day nestles the Higher Man of the future—The first last, and the last first—Growth always accompanied with pain—Co-operation with the law makes growth less painful—Folly of opposing growth—The Something Within is pressing for unfoldment.

Man's development has been along the lines of a gradual unfoldment of consciousness. I call your attention to the fact that I speak of *unfoldment*, rather than acquirement, although the process of growth and development includes both the unfoldment, or growth from within, and the acquirement, or growth from without. There is something within that exerts a steady urge in the direction of unfoldment, and there is an attracting power that draws to one, and appropriates that which is needed from outside. It will be remembered, of course, that I use the words *within*, and without, in the relative sense, recognizing fully the fact that from the Absolute point of view within and without are one and the same thing.

There is in each of us a mighty force pressing forth for expression and growth in the direction of the ultimate Good—impelling us to unfold and develop—casting off sheath after sheath in its progressive development and unfoldment—impelled by the impulse imparted by the Causeless Cause—attracted upward by the attraction of the Absolute. Like a plant, we are impelled to grow on slowly, but surely—steadily—from seed to blossom—until our potentialities are fully expressed. We grow as does the lily, freely and steadily, unfolding leaf after leaf, until the plant stands in its complete beauty, crowned with its divine flower.

There is in the center of our being a Something which directs a mighty urge toward unfoldment and development, and we will follow these impulses so long as there remains within us one atom of Life. The seed in the ground will express itself in its little shoot, often moving weights a thousand times heavier than itself in its efforts to reach the rays of the sun. The sapling may be bent and confined to the ground but its branches, following the laws of its being, will instinctively shoot upward, moving along the lines of least resistance, and growing toward the sun, in spite of all efforts to restrict it. Like the plant—like the sapling—this Something within us will not allow us to submit to the confining bonds—will not allow us to conform to the false standards set up for our observance from time to time. Submitting as long as it must, it stores up reserve strength day by day, keeping up a continuous pressure in the direction of its desire, until some day, by a supreme effort, it throws off the restraining obstacles, and, obeying the laws of its being, again grows toward the sun.

Life is growth. It moves along, pressing this way and that way, along the lines of least resistance, drawing to itself that which it needs today, and discarding it tomorrow, after it has served its purpose, after its helpful qualities have been extracted. It assumes many forms in its growth, discarding sheath after sheath when outgrown. Any attempt to compel it to retain a sheath which has become outgrown, will cause the life-nature to revolt, and, in the end, with a mighty effort, it will burst forth, tearing the restraining sheath into fragments.

The philosophic mind, considering the great questions underlying Life, soon is brought in contact with what has been called the Divine Paradox. He finds himself forced to recognize apparently conflicting aspects of the same thing—finds two equally satisfactory answers to the same question, either of which would suit were it not for the other. This state of affairs places the philosopher in the position of being able to answer any great question relatively by either "Yes," or "No." And yet if the Center is once recognized, the philosopher sees not only that *neither* answer is strictly correct (speaking from the absolute position), but that *both* answers combined give the only approach to a correct answer. One is forced to answer: "It is and it isn't." The explanation is partially understood when we remember that no absolute truth can be conveyed in relative terms. This Divine Paradox confronts the novitiate entering the Path. Do not let it frighten you off—it is terrible only in appearance—when you know it well you see that it is a friend and a helper.

This Divine Paradox confronts us when we come to consider the question of the growth, development and unfoldment of Man. One set of thinkers will contend that Man grows and develops only by causes external to himself—that he is a creature of heredity, environment, circumstances. Another school will teach that his growth is entirely from within, and that external causes have no effect whatever upon him. Both will confront you with

splendid arguments, striking illustrations and examples, and
for the moment you are almost convinced, until the other side
of the question occurs to you. Then you are torn with contradictions, and unless you recognize the Divine Paradox, you
will finally be forced into the position of saying: "I do not
know."

There are two general causes operating in the development of
the Ego—one internal, and the other external. These causes
are, from the relative position, conflicting; from the absolute, one.
Neither of these relative causes determines or controls the development of Man. There is a constant play or reaction of these two
forces. The internal urge meets with numerous obstacles, hin·
drances, barriers and obstructions, which, apparently, turn aside
the Ego from its path laid out for it by the Power Within.
And yet, the inner force urges forward and either surmounts,
overcomes, climbs over, undermines, or passes around the ex·
ternal obstacle. It might, at first glance seem like the old propo·
sition of "the irresistible force coming in contact with the immov·
able body", which proposition is beyond the understanding of the
mind of man, but the comparison is not exact, because whilst the
two forces continually play one upon the other, the inner urge
modified by the external hindrances is in the end victorious, and
the plant of Life rises toward the sun. The mighty river on its
way to the ocean, was forced to turn this way and that way—
forced to bend here and tunnel there—but in the end the ocean
was reached, and the water of the river reached home at last.

I wish to say here that my philosophy teaches me that in the
final analysis the internal force and the opposing obstacle will be
seen as but different manifestations of one thing, and that in the
apparent inharmony is to be found the highest form of harmony.
In speaking of relative things, one must use relative terms in
order to be understood at all. In fact, if one wished to speak
solely from the absolute position, he would find no words to express himself, and would be forced to remain mute. I say this
now, in order that I may not be misunderstood later. For the purpose of delivering my message, I must assume that this inner
force, urging toward unfoldment, is the prime factor in man's
advancement, and that the external forces playing upon that inner
force are in the nature of obstacles. I trust, however, before we
are through with each other, to cause you to see that both are vital
factors in the *development* of Man.

One feature of this process of unfoldment is most necessary to
remember, and that is that the final, or ultimate, effect or product,
is practically the underlying cause of the unfoldment itself. The
blossom or the fruit urging for expression, causes the seed to
sprout, the plant to grow a stalk, put forth leaves and fufill all

the laws of its growth. The potential oak within the acorn, eager for expression, causes the entire growth and development of the tree. In the lowest form of Life was to be found the potential Man, urging for expression and development through millions of years. Man the effect, was Man the cause. The last to appear, in point of time, was the first in point of cause. And in Man of today nestles the potential Higher Man of the future, and perhaps beyond him in ascending order beings as much superior to Man as man is to the lowest form of life known to science. Verily, "the first shall be last, and the last shall be first", in more senses than one.

In looking at a growing plant, or flower, one is apt to be impressed at the ease and naturalness of the growth—at the absence of effort or pain, and we may wonder why this process is not carried out in the higher forms of development. We wonder why Man cannot develop his Ego in like manner, without all the pains of growth, struggle and effort. Alas, we are blind. Could we but look at the plant through a sufficiently large and strong microscope, we would see there a continual tearing down and building up—destruction—effort—pain—tearing asunder—discarding—replacing. Change—change always. But the plant, true to the instincts of nature, does not needlessly oppose the laws of its growth, and pain is reduced to a minimum, and may even afford a certain sense of pleasure (for pain and pleasure are not so far apart), but Man seems to oppose each step of growth, and holds himself in, fearing the change and prolonging and intensifying his pain. Poor Man—but he is learning.

We will have more to say about this process of unfoldment in other parts of this book, and will leave the subject for the present, in order to take up the different forms of Man's unfoldment. Carry this in your minds, however, that there is Something Within, pressing forth for development and unfoldment. And that Something is that which will in the end appear as the divine flower upon our plant of Life. It is not a thing foreign to us— not something from the outside—but is the Higher Self, which will one day be what we mean when we say "I". At present the "I" is our consciousness of the highest stage of our present development. Your "I" of today, is far different from your "I" of ten years ago, and your "I" of ten years from now will be far different from your "I" of today. And when we realize that this process is to be continued throughout ages, our reasoning powers fail us for the moment—we cannot grasp this wondrous truth, pregnant with such marvelous possibilities.

CHAPTER XV.

THE GROWTH OF CONSCIOUSNESS.

Consciousness in the lower animals—Mere sensation at first; almost auto-matic—Growth—Lower form of Consciousness—The development of Self-consciousness—Definition of Simple Consciousness and Self-consciousness—The first conception of the "I"—"I" on the physical plane—An animal happiness—All his troubles before him—The mental plane—"I" as the intellect—Worshiping Intellect as God—Different forms of mental development—Psychic development—' Man's suffering begins when he reaches the mental plane of develop-ment—Dissatisfaction and anxiety—Hemmed in at all sides—The eternal "Why"—No answer to the demands of the intellect—The only possible avenue of escape.

It is important to understand something about the growth and development of consciousness in Man—the unfoldment of the "I" consciousness within him.

In the lower order of animals there is a very small amount of what we call consciousness. The consciousness of the lower forms of life is little more than mere sensation—the subconscious plane of life is in the ascendant, and even that upon only the grosser faculties, the higher faculties remaining dormant and un-developed. Life in the lower forms is almost automatic. In the mineral world there appears to be no life at all, so almost com-pletely is the life principle smothered in matter. And yet the oc-cultists tell us that even in the mineral world there is the first faint indication of life, and some of the more advanced scientists are beginning to recognize that matter is not entirely dead—that there is nothing absolutely dead in Nature—that intelligence is merely a matter of degree—that the mineral has its law of life which it follows.

There is in Nature an instinctive tendency of living organisms to perform certain actions—the tendency of an organized body to seek that which satisfies the wants of its organism. It is a simple form of mental effort, apparently wholly along sub-conscious lines. In plant life this tendency is plainly discernible, ranging from the lesser exhibitions in the lower types, to the greater in the higher types. It is this which is often spoken of as the "life force" in plants. In some of the higher forms of plant life, how-ever, there appears a faint color of independent "life action"—a faint indication of consciousness—a faint exhibition of conscious effort.

In the lower animal kingdom, we see a much higher grade of consciousness, varying in degree in the several family and species, from the almost plant-like forms of the lowest animal forms to the almost human intelligence of the highest forms. The degree of consciousness in the highest of the so-called "lower animals", almost approaches that of the lowest form of the human race, and certainly reaches that of the young child. As a child, before birth, shows in its body the stages of physical evolution of Man; so does a child, before and after birth—until maturity—manifest the stages of the *mental* evolution of Man.

As Man progressed in development and unfoldment, he began to manifest the first indications of what is known as Self Consciousness, which is higher in the scale than Simple Consciousness. It is very difficult to convey in words the idea of consciousness in its different forms, in fact many writers on psychology state that, strictly speaking, it is incapable of definition. To describe a thing it is necessary to compare it with something else, and as there is nothing else in nature like consciousness, we have nothing with which we can compare it. To my mind the best idea of consciousness is conveyed by the words: "awareness"; "knowing".

Simple consciousness is an awareness of *outward* things—of things other than the inner self. Self-consciousness is an awareness of the *inner* self—a result of turning the mental gaze *inward*. The great majority of people scarcely know what self-consciousness is. They are in the habit of taking themselves as a matter of course, and never deem it necessary to take mental stock of themselves. On the other hand some become morbidly self-conscious, and find it difficult to turn their gaze away from themselves. It is the old principle of the outer and inner, which manifests itself in so many forms.

With the advent of Self-consciousness, came to Man a conception of the "I". Heretofore he had never formed the mental concept "I". At first the concept was hazy and dim. Man began to think of himself as compared to others of his kind. He began to notice himself, make deductions the results of which he applied to others. The concept of "I" began to grow. Let us leave primitive man, in whom this "I" realization is unfolding, and come down to man of today. A little thought will show us that each of us has an "I" in a different stage of development. We think of ourselves in different ways.

Many of us think of ourselves on the physical plane alone. We think of the "I" as a physical being, having a head, body, limbs and organs ranging from brain to liver. To one in this stage of development, the Body is the real self, and the Mind but a dimly understood appendage of the Body—something necessary for the uses of the body. Such a man speaks of "my mind" or "my soul", as things belonging to him (the Body) and which he uses, but which are not *him*. To him "my mind" or "my soul" are but as "my hat", "my coat", "my shoes"—something attached to or used, but not "I". The "I" is on the physical plane alone, the higher part of the man is his "not I", just as are the things he wears or otherwise uses.

The man on the physical plane lives the physical life. He eats, drinks, sleeps, and performs other physical acts which come easy and seem pleasant to him. He finds his sole pleasure in the physical—he knows nothing else. His emotions and passions are but slightly in advance of the brute and he fails to understand another man who has grown beyond this stage. Of course we cannot blame such a man, or condemn him, for he can only see what he is, and if we were in his stage of development, we would do just the same. It is a necessary stage of development, through which each has passed, or is passing. It is the childhood stage. Such a man is like a young bear—all his troubles are before him. He has a comparatively easy time—the only pain he recognizes is pain to the body, or what is its equivalent, a deprivation of that which would gratify the sensual nature. He does not realize that his is not the highest life, and he feels a sense of pity or contempt for those who find pleasure in other things. He enjoys a sort of animal happiness, and it seems to be rather a pity that he has to be awakened, and face the pain of the next stage—but Life is inexorable—the child must grow, in spite of pain—yes, by means of pain.

Some of us have grown out of the physical stage of consciousness, into the mental stage. To one who has reached this plane, the "I" is pictured as Intellect, or Mind, having control of the body and its organs, and having its abode in the brain or brains of the human being. It makes very little difference whether these people think of Mind as does the materialist—a substance evolved from, or secreted by, the brain; or whether they regard it as a somewhat intangible substance manifesting through the brain. Either view is a matter of Intellectual opinion with them, and they *feel* the same in either case—in either case their picture of the "I" is the same—they have a feeling that the center of their consciousness is in the Intellect. To such a man the Intellect seems to be the real self, in fact he may even get to the point where he will bow down to his Intellect and worship it as a God. He realizes the wonderful powers of the mind, and begins to cultivate and develop them (all of which is a very necessary part of growth) and often attains results little short of marvelous. Some of these men will follow the path of pure Intellectual abstraction; others will develop the creative power of the mind, and manifest it in wonderful inventions, great discoveries, etc.; others will develop the Imagination, and become poets, writers, artists; others will combine the operative and imaginative qualities, and become "captains of industry," etc., etc. Each will follow the line of least resistance and will develop upon lines which prove more attractive, but their "I" is always the Mind. Some will proceed along certain lines of psychic development, which is merely one form of manifestation along the mental plane. Psychic power is by many considered to be identical with spiritual power, but is really on the mental plane of consciousness, although the higher form of psychic power is available only to those who have attained a certain stage of spiritual development. The lower forms of psychic power may be acquired by those who develop the mind along certain lines, and they belong strictly to the mental plane, although apparently far removed from ordinary mental development. The higher forms of psychic power can be attained only by those who have reached a certain stage of spiritual unfoldment.

To the men on the Mental plane, the Mind is all. They realize its mastery of the body; are aware of the wonderful powers of the Mind over the particular body under its control; the bodies of others; the minds of others. To them the Mind is the highest self—identical with Spirit. They are conscious of the wonderful workings of the Mind, but are conscious of nothing higher. To some of them death seems to end all, their idea being that all dies with the brain. Others feel, somehow, that their Intellect will maintain its existence, but it is merely a *belief* or hope, based upon the words or opinions of others who have claimed authority to speak. But they have no *awareness* of Eternal Life—no perception of the Real Self which *knows* itself to be Eternal.

When a man enters fully upon the mental plane of consciousness, his troubles commence. He grows dissatisfied. He feels new longings, which he strives to satisfy. Tolstoi says of this state: "As soon as the mental part of a person takes control, new worlds are opened, and desires are multiplied a thousand-fold. They become as numerous as the radii of a circle; and the mind, with care and axiety, sets itself first to cultivate and then gratify these desires, thinking that happiness is to be had in that way." But although the mental stage brings its own happiness, it brings its own pains and unhappiness. Man finds himself hemmed in at all quarters by the limits of the Intellect. He crys: "Why?" And he finds no answer in the enclosure of his intellect. He grows beyond accepting things just because someone else has said them, and he demands an answer of his reasoning faculties— he directs his Intellect to lead him, but he finds out after a while that the Intellect is leading him a wearisome journey round and round a well worn path, and he finds himself far away from that which he seeks. The further Man advances along purely Intellectual lines, the more unhappiness he opens himself up to. The more he suffers the more he knows. And yet Intellect is the finest tool with which the Spirit works, and when one attains the higher stages of consciousness—enters the realm of Spiritual Consciousness, he takes great delight in wielding the polished weapon of the Intellect, not in the old way but as a valuable instrument in the hands of the Spirit.

Man's only possible escape from the pain of the mental plane is through the channel of spiritual unfoldment—the growth of consciousness along spiritual lines—the turning of the light of consciousness into the heretofore unexplored field of the spiritual faculties. Here alone is peace.

In the next chapter I will speak of the spiritual unfoldment.

CHAPTER XVI.

THE SOUL'S AWAKENING.

The Pilgrim on The Path—The path among the hills—An unknown road
—One step at a time—A strange land—No landmarks—A stopping
place and point of observation—A wondrous view—The awakening
of the Spiritual Consciousness—The knowing of the "I Am"—Consciousness of immortality—Consciousness of one's place in the Universe—Recognition of one's relation to other parts of the Whole—
The border-land of the Cosmic Knowing—A tiny drop of Spirit
from the Great Spirit Ocean—Recognition of the Universal Presence
—Seeing things as they are—God's sunshine and his love, bestowed
upon all—The "Lost Sheep" now understood—Treading the Path—
The Soul's Awakening—Joy! Joy! Joy!—The song of the Soul.

Man has progressed along the Lines of unfoldment, growth and
development, traveling, in turn, through the stages of the physical
plane, then into the large and broader mental plane in all its
varied phases. From the comparatively care-free physical plane,
he has passed on to the mental plane with all its worries, doubts,
struggles, agnosticism, denial, longings, dissatisfaction, unhappiness. Finally he sees a new path winding up the hills, and although he knows not where it leads, he, in despair, seeks to travel
it, hoping, almost against hope, that it may lead him to the Promised Land of Peace.

He travels along. He notices the marks of the feet of those
who have traveled before, but sees also that but few have traveled that path. He feels doubtful, for instead of being able to
see whither the road leads him, he finds that the path is winding,
and he can see scarcely more than a few steps ahead. But carried on by a longing which he scarcely comprehends, he takes the
few steps with faith in his heart, and having taken them he is
conscious of ascending the hills, and other steps open up before
him. He remembers the words of the old, familiar hymn:

> * * * * "I do not ask to see the distant scene;
> One step enough for me. Lead Thou me on."

Soon he becomes conscious that he has entered into a new and
unknown land—has crossed the borders of a new country. He
finds himself in a strange land—there are no familiar landmarks
—he does not recognize the scene. He realizes the great distance
between himself and the friends he has left at the foot of the hill.
He cries aloud for them to follow him, but they can scarcely hear

him, and seem to fear for his safety. They wave their arms, and
beckon with their hands for him to return. They fear to follow
him, and despair of his safety. But he seems possessed of a new
courage, and a strange impulse within him urges him on and on.
To what point he is traveling, he knows not, but a fierce joy takes
possession of him, and he presses on and on and on.

After a bit, when he has traveled a particularly difficult bit of
road, he comes to a turn of the path, and steps forward upon a
broad bit of flat ground, which gives him a feeling of rest—he
knows it as a stopping place—a stage for halting and observation. He finds that he has a wondrous view. On one side he can
see those on the plains below, striving this way and that way in a
pitiful manner—seeking to progress. Away back on various paths
he sees men and women struggling on, and strange to say he instinctively feels and realizes that they are all seeking for the path
upon which he has entered and which he has followed for a little
way. On the other side he sees a beautiful, new country—a land
of sunshine and brightness. He sees, afar off, groups of people,
traveling up the higher paths of the journey, and, borne from afar,
the sound of their voices reach him—they are singing with joy.
He feels for the first time what the real "I" is. He recognizes
both body and mind as useful instruments, tools, servants, but he
has a distinct recognition of the "I" apart from them, and using
them.

He becomes conscious of having always existed—existing now
—and being intended for existence forever. He does not reason
out these things—he knows them, just as before he had felt that
he existed at any particular moment. The "I Am" has taken on
a new meaning—has apparently grown, although he knows that
it has not really grown, but that he for the first time has arrived
at a stage of consciousness capable of recognizing himself as
he is.

He knows that he has traveled a long road leading to his present position, and that he has a long journey before him, but from
now on he will travel knowingly, and not blindly. He looks down
and sees others covered with the mire and dust of the road, traveling on the plane below, but knowing that he too has traveled the
same paths, he does not condemn them for the mire and dust.
He has shared their journey with all its discomfort and dirt. He
knows that he is in but the borderland of the Cosmic Knowing—
and that beyond lie regions of marvelous beauty which in turn
will be traveled. He sees endless phases of existence opening up
to the vision.

The Soul when it reaches this stage, awakens, and sees itself
as it is, in all its beauty—with all its wonderful possibilities. It
feels a keen pleasure in existence—in the NOW. It feels itself

to be a part of the WHOLE—knows that the Universe is its home. It knows itself to be a tiny drop of Spirit from the Great Spirit Ocean—a ray from the Supreme Sun—a particle of Divine Being, encased in a material body, using that body and something called mind, with which to manifest itself. It frets not about the Past —it worries not about the Future. It realizes that it IS and always will be, and therefore lives in the NOW. It knows that it cannot be injured or destroyed—that it exists in accordance with Law (and that Law is Good). It seeks no explanation, knowing that as the time comes, it will progress through matter, discarding sheath after sheath in its unfoldment, attaining greater and greater degrees of knowing.

It recognizes the existence of The Universal Presence—it becomes aware of GOD and his nearness. It realizes for the first time the reality of that which it had so glibly spoken of before, but never with understanding—the Omnipresence, Omnipotence, and Omniscience of GOD. And seeing and knowing these things —it is content. And it sees its Oneness with All. It knows that progress for one means progress for all—that no one part of the Whole is separate from the Whole, or from any part of the Whole. It sees these things, and is amazed. Seeing these things the feelings of the old life—Hate, Fear, Envy, Jealousy, Malice—drop from it. It cannot Despise or Condemn. It sees Ignorance instead of Evil. It sees Separateness and Selfishness, where before it saw sin. It finds itself possessed of but one feeling toward Mankind and the whole world—Love. Aye, Love for the lowest creature that exists—for the vilest man—the most degraded woman—for it knows that even these cannot be left out of the grand scheme of Life, and that even these cannot escape their good, eventually. And it feels its relationship and connection with all Life—knows them to be inseparably connected—and knows that what is good for the one is for the good of all, and that what hurts the one, hurts all.

It sees that GOD'S love extends to all, no matter how far back on the path they may be. It sees that GOD'S Love—like GOD'S sunshine—is bestowed upon all alike—Saint and Sinner partaking of both. It sees that there is no living creature so humble, or so sunk in the mire of ignorance, but that GOD still remembers it, and is ready and anxious to lend a helping hand, and that sooner or later the helping hand will be grasped by the unfortunate, and he will be raised up. It realizes for the first time what means the parable of "The Lost Sheep", and it sighs to think how little it had grasped of its meaning, in the old life.

It sees Death and Life as one. It sees Death as Birth. It loses all its fear of Death, knowing it as it is. It sees behind the hideous mask of Death, the beautiful face of the radiant creature—Life.

These and other experiences come to the Soul when it awakens. And it does not stop seeing, for new visions come to it continually, and its eyes become clearer from time to time. Life takes on a new meaning when one reaches the borders of Spiritual Consciousness, and takes a few steps beyond the borders. Words cannot convey the idea—it must be experienced to be comprehended. You are perhaps at the foot of the hill—at the beginning of the narrow path. You can see but the first step—take it, take it. Never mind the steps beyond—they will be seen by you when you are ready for them. Step boldly forth upon the Path, and look not backward. The Path is narrow and winding, but it has been trodden by the Elect of all the ages, and many are ready for it now. You may find it necessary to cast aside many worthless things which you are now carrying—much that is really a burden to you, but to which you have been clinging as if it were most precious. Prejudices—narrowness—hates—dislikes—enviousness—feelings of superiority to your brethren—lack of charity for others—condemnation—bigotry—worn-out husks of sheaths which have reached the period of discarding—forms—musty and mouldy ideas, heirlooms from the past—self-righteousness—these and other useless things will impede your progress, and will be cast aside one by one as you proceed up The Path. Things which you have been carrying around and upon which you have prided yourself very much, will be seen as worse than worthless, and will be thrown aside with relief, although at first with pain. Much finery with which you have bedecked yourself, will be torn from you by the stones and thorns of the road, or will be discarded as too heavy for the shoulders to carry. Yes, and after you have reached the higher stages of the journey, you will be glad to discard all of the clothing with which you have tried to cover the spirit, and finally the Soul will stand forth naked and beautiful and not ashamed.

See! the light is stealing over the hills, and the rays of the rising sun have penetrated your chamber and are shining full upon your face. You are shaking off the weight of the heavy sleep— you feel the drowsiness of the half-waking state. Open your eyes —great things are before you today—rise from your couch, and go to your window, and let the bright health-giving rays of the sun fall upon you. All seems beautiful to you—Life is worth the living—the hideous visions of the night have flown—you are at last wide awake and smiling. You hear the voice of the Soul singing "Joy! Joy! Joy!" It is the hour of the Soul's Awakening.

Description of NT
Law of attraction
conscious, subconscious, superconscious
God as One & all-encompassing:
    Substance
    Energy
    Spirit
Theosophical influ - Bulwer Lytton & Zanoni
Thought waves & public opinion
Desire, delight, joy